Cycling Across America in 101 Poems
—
A Stroke Recovery Journey

MICHAEL OBEL-OMIA

ALSO BY
MICHAEL OBEL-OMIA

Finding My Words: Aphasia Poetry

Cycling Across America in 101 Poems

A Stroke Recovery Journey

MICHAEL OBEL-OMIA

Cycling Across America in 101 Poems: A Stroke Recovery Journey
Copyright © 2025 Michael Obel-Omia

Produced and printed by Stillwater River Publications.
All rights reserved. Written and produced in the United States of America. This book may not be reproduced or sold in any form without the expressed, written permission of the author(s) and publisher.

Visit our website at **www.StillwaterPress.com** for more information.

First Stillwater River Publications Edition.

ISBN: 978-1-968548-32-2

Library of Congress Control Number: 2025927281

1 2 3 4 5 6 7 8 9 10

Written by Michael Obel-Omia.
Cover photograph by Michael Obel Omia.
Cover & interior book design by Matthew St. Jean.
Published by Stillwater River Publications, West Warwick, RI, USA.

Publisher's Cataloging-in-Publication
(Provided by Cassidy Cataloguing Services, Inc.)

Names: Obel-Omia, Michael, author, illustrator.
Title: Cycling across America in 101 poems : a stroke recovery journey / Michael Obel-Omia.
Description: First Stillwater River Publications edition. | West Warwick, RI, USA : Stillwater River Publications, [2026]
Identifiers: LCCN: 2025927281 | ISBN: 9781968548322
Subjects: LCSH: Cycling—United States. | Cerebrovascular disease—Patients—Travel—United States. | Landscapes—United States. | Friendship. | Resilience (Personality trait) | United States—Description and travel. | LCGFT: Poetry.
Classification: LCC: PS3615.B41 C93 2026 | DDC: 811/.6—dc23

The views and opinions expressed in this book are solely those of the author(s) and do not necessarily reflect the views and opinions of the publisher.

*To my wife Carolyn, for her endless support,
patience, comfort, and inspiration.*

Contents

Introduction ... xi

POEM 1	Anticipation	1
POEM 2	Doubting Thomas	2
POEM 3	Haiku	3
POEM 4	Have You Ever Seen The Rain?	4
POEM 5	Empowered	5
POEM 6	Big Sky	6
POEM 7	Dillon to Alder, Montana	7
POEM 8	Alder to Ennis	8
POEM 9	Earthquake Lake	9
POEM 10	A rest day in Idaho	10
POEM 11	One Full Week, Yellowstone to Aston, ID	12
POEM 12	Ashton to Victor, Idaho	14
POEM 13	A Storm Coming	15
POEM 14	28 miles uphill	16
POEM 15	Grand Tetons	17
POEM 16	Odyssey	18
POEM 17	Wyoming Winds	19
POEM 18	I'm so tired	20
POEM 19	Juneteeth	21
POEM 20	Rawlins, Wyoming	22
POEM 21	Interstate 80	23
POEM 22	A Fall	24
POEM 23	That fought with us upon Saint Crispin's day "Riverside to Walden, Colorado"	25
POEM 24	"Cameron Pass, 10,276 feet"	26
POEM 25	Boulder, Colorado	28
POEM 26	A Haven in Boulder, Colorado	29
POEM 27	Stroke Onward Event, Sterne Park	30

POEM 28	Boulder to Boyd Lake State Park	31
POEM 29	Briggsdale, Colorado	32
POEM 30	Briggsdale to Sterling 58 Miles	33
POEM 31	Sterling, Colorado, Zero miles	34
POEM 32	The Good Samaritan	35
POEM 33	Sterling, Colorado to Holyoke, Colorado	36
POEM 34	Holyoke, Colorado to Imperial, Nebraska	37
POEM 35	Imperial, Nebraska to McCook, Nebraska	38
POEM 36	75 miles McCook to Alma, Nebraska Independence Day	39
POEM 37	Through hardship to the stars Alma, Nebraska to Smith Center, Kansas	40
POEM 38	"Bellevue, Kansas, it's Hot"	41
POEM 39	Nothing today, Laundry Day	43
POEM 40	Belleville, Kansas to Marysville, Kansas	44
POEM 41	The Crash	45
POEM 42	Goodbye, Sandra	46
POEM 43	Kansas, The Sunflower State	47
POEM 44	Time passes in Kansas	48
POEM 45	I'll be back	49
POEM 46	"Kansas City to KMBC, Kansas, an Event"	50
POEM 47	Comeback	51
POEM 48	From Windsor to Boonville, 60 miles	52
POEM 49	Boonville, to Jefferson City, 59 Miles	53
POEM 50	Jefferson City—No Cycling	54
POEM 51	Katy Trail State Park, Jefferson to Hermann	55
POEM 52	"Hermann to Augusta, 39.1 miles"	56
POEM 53	Stories of the land "Augusta to St. Louis, 58 miles"	57
POEM 54	"The Show Me State"	59
POEM 55	"An Event in St. Louis, Gateway Arch"	60
POEM 56	St. Louis, Missouri to Litchfield, Illinois	62
POEM 57	I am content	63

POEM 58	Springfield to Goodfield, 77 Miles	64
POEM 59	A rainy day in Goodfield, Illinois: Three Songs	65
POEM 60	Father-in-law	66
POEM 61	"Dwight, Illinois to Joliet, Illinois, 66 Miles"	67
POEM 62	Sweet Home, Chicago- "A Guardian Angel"	68
POEM 63	"Gothic Art, the Beam, Chicago Event"	69
POEM 64	"Land of Lincoln"	71
POEM 65	"Route 66"	73
POEM 66	Gary, Indiana	74
POEM 67	"Indiana Dunes National Park"	75
POEM 68	"Michigan City, IN to South Haven, MI"	76
POEM 69	"South Haven, Augusta, Michigan 52 Miles"	77
POEM 70	Augusta, to Concord, Michigan, 53 miles	78
POEM 71	"One"	79
POEM 72	"Concord, to Ann Arbor, MI 66 Miles"	80
POEM 73	Laundry, New Cycling Shoes, an Event	82
POEM 74	"Ann Arbor to Rochester, Michigan"	84
POEM 75	An Event in Detroit, Corktown	86
POEM 76	Rochester, MI to Algonac, MI 59 Miles	87
POEM 77	"Morpeth, Ontario to Port Burwell, ON, 73 miles"	90
POEM 78	Migraine, Right There	91
POEM 79	Port Burwell, Canada, Laundry, 0 miles	92
POEM 80	Port Burwell to Port Dover, 44 Miles	93
POEM 81	Port Dover, to Dunville Ontario, 49 miles	94
POEM 82	Thinking back: where we've been	95
POEM 83	Canada	97
POEM 84	"Dunville, Ontario to Buffalo, New York 40 miles"	98
POEM 85	Event, Buffalo, New York	99
POEM 86	"Buffalo to Niagara Falls, 34 miles"	100
POEM 87	Erie Canal	101

POEM 88	Spencerport to Clyde, NY 68 Miles	102
POEM 89	Bridgeport, NY to Herkimer, NY 63 Miles	104
POEM 90	Event, Albany: Carolyn will be there!	105
POEM 91	Herkimer NY to Schenectady NY, 66 Miles	106
POEM 92	Schenectady to Castleton, NY, 47 Miles	107
POEM 93	New York	108
POEM 94	Castleton, NY to Pittsfield, MA 39 Miles	110
POEM 95	Pittsfield to Northhampton, MA, 50 miles	111
POEM 96	North Hampton, MA to West Brookfield, MA	112
POEM 97	West Brookfield, MA to Concord, MA, 55 Miles	113
POEM 98	Massachusetts	114
POEM 99	Revere Beach	116
POEM 100	Ode to Steve and Debra	117

Introduction

Before my stroke, I was an athlete. I played football in high school and rugby in college. I ran the Boston Marathon twice and cycled in many road races. I regularly cycled 50- or 100-mile bike fundraisers. I even rode my bike across the country from Anaheim, California to New York City.

On the morning of Saturday, 21 May 2016, I was lying in bed, planning my day, and suddenly, I felt like I was drowning. I tried to catch my breath. Carolyn, my beloved wife, asked, "Michael, are you all right?" Thrashing through the sheets and covers, I waved my hands, but I couldn't say anything. "Michael, get up! If you don't get up, I'll call 9-1-1!"

I kept thrashing, and I couldn't speak—I wanted to answer her, to tell her to give me time, but I couldn't speak, I just couldn't speak. The EMT was talking to me, asking questions, but I shook my head, and I waved him off: I just wanted to sleep. They put me in a stretcher and carried me downstairs: as I was pulled away, even though I couldn't speak, I managed to call out, "My iPhone, I need my iPhone!"

In the Rhode Island Hospital emergency room, Jackson, my oldest son, was there. I grabbed his hand, and I mumbled, tightly gripping his hand, "I'll be alright, and I love you." I fell asleep and then woke up, in and out. Each time I awoke, someone else was there. I tried to talk to them, to make them understand that I had to go home and get ready to chaperone a group of students to Washington, D.C. But, instead of saying that, I repeatedly said, "May I please have tomorrow?" I asked everyone, again and again, "May I please have tomorrow?" Confused, they said, "Yes, you may have tomorrow." But they did not understand.

After 48 hours at Rhode Island Hospital, I was taken to Spaulding Rehabilitation in Charlestown, MA. Strapped to a stretcher, I was carried to the van and then to my new home for the next 37 days - the 6th floor of Spaulding Rehabilitation Hospital. For 37 days, I wanted to get out. They wouldn't let me go anywhere unless I was in the wheelchair. They wanted me to ring for help when I went to the bathroom, but I learned how to turn the bed alarm off and go by myself. In addition to extensive work with the speech therapist and OT, I worked each day with the PT. I was miserable. One day, she wheeled me to the gym and asked me to walk across the mat to practice walking on an uneven surface. When I got to the end of the mat - a whopping 6 feet - she started clapping. I was infuriated. Seething, I held my tongue. After 37 days, I was "set free" from Spaulding.

When I got home, I was determined to cycle. Before my stroke, on a bike, I felt light and free. I wanted that feeling again. When cycling, I didn't have to work to put words together or to comprehend words. I just rode. I had ridden the Rodman Ride for Kids for many years and the race was coming up in September. I was determined. I rode my stationary bike and a three-wheeled recumbent trike that a friend lent me. That was not good enough. I finally got on my road bike, and, with my dear friend Karin Wetherill, rode 1.5 miles. I rode to the YMCA, 0.7 miles away, and fell down twice. I rode home and fell down three more times. I was despondent and depressed. But I was determined, improving, always improving. I kept riding on the stationary bike and riding outside for short rides. On Saturday, 25 September 2016, 4 months after my stroke, I did it. With an entourage of friends and family surrounding me, I rode 25 miles for the Rodman Ride for Kids.

Eventually, I had the opportunity to meet Debra Myerson through Boston University Aphasia Resource Center. This led me to learn of the Stroke across America bike ride, in which I cycled 3,383 miles from Missoula, Montana to Revere Beach, Massachusetts. I overcame rain, heat, cold, and yes, camping. And I only fell off my bike 3 times! I had to do it. I set my mind on the task and rode 3,383 miles until I walked into the Atlantic Ocean, holding my bike over my head in victory. After completing the ride, some of us rode over to Spaulding Rehabilitation for a reception. Biking to Spaulding and standing at the podium, sharing my story about riding over 3,000 miles at the same place where I had been applauded for walking only 6 feet, made me realize - I'm back.

I was an athlete and I still am an athlete. Improving, always improving.

POEM 1: 1 JUNE 2022
Anticipation

In the solstice, dreary, doldrums, cold time,
I rowed: no problem, 100 days, ha!
Looking outside in the dark, wintry time,
I thought I could row hard and cycle, too:
100 days, yes, I can lose some weight!
In March, in April, in May, now in June,
I'm flying, in the air, and I'm nervous:
Those March days? I cycled cold, & wintry.
Those April days? I cycled still, I rowed.
In May, I cycled, longer rides
And now, I can feel the plane descending, Denver below
It's bright with beautiful mountains, rivers
Missoula will be next; I'm anxious.
72 hours until I ride.
87 days ahead: just do it!

POEM 2: 2 JUNE 2022
Doubting Thomas

Christ opened the doors, and they marveled
Now Thomas, one of the twelve, was there.
Doubtful, chary, Thomas was wary
"We have seen the Lord, you have missed him, friend"
Skeptical, unsure, Thomas. Unconvinced:
"Until I see the nail marks in his hands,
And put my fingers where the nails were now,
Then my doubting friend, I will believe!"
Ah, aphasia, the invisible loss.
I can imagine, trying to believe,
But, every word leaves me trying, feckless.
You can believe me, don't you? I'm trying.
Ah, Jesus, came and stood: Peace be with you!
Astonished, doubting Thomas made it true.
Yes, stroke does bring doubt into my life:
You may doubt me, until you see, I will cycle.

POEM 3: 3 JUNE 2022
Haiku

No cycling, rest up.
Beautiful paintings, so nice
Quiet day, stunning.

POEM 4: 4 JUNE 2022
Have You Ever Seen The Rain?

April is the cruelest month and Montana
While cycling east, it rained, poured, deluged
For every tug, it rained, 66 miles,
It was pouring, dripping from my wet helmet,
Fogging my eyeglasses, while I churned, burned
But, look at the sight, majestic mountains,
Water swelling the rivers, streams, creeks,
Around that flow, Florence, Darby lie ahead.
I felt the misty mountains around me,
And I knew, I will ride ahead, cycling

POEM 5: 5 JUNE 2022
Empowered

With a stroke, surround yourself with this:
Empower yourself to strive and rise up.
Believe in yourself, who will work and try
Support yourself through a stroke: don't give up
Uplift yourself now, with an attitude
Motivate yourself with perseverance
Appreciate yourself: you can do this!

> *"Our greatest glory is not in never falling, but in getting up every time we fall."* —Confucius

POEM 6: 6 JUNE 2022
Big Sky

On a Monday, cycling across this land
I'm anxious, Dillon, Montana today
Yesterday, I had a frustrating day,
Snowy, rainy, cold, icy, failing, lost
Today again, raining, windy, really?
But the rainbow could be a harbinger.
Cycling 66 miles, sunny, let's go!
12 disciples, it seems, we'll do this ride
Montana, big sky, couldn't be better
Jackson, Montana, my son, picture it!
Beautiful day, cycling, chatting – perfect!
Uphill, oh boy, two miles straight, can I do that?
Struggling, again, huge winds, come on!
Suddenly, downhill, 35 miles straight,
"He tends his flock, like a shepherd," gliding
Together, in the sunny, windy, cold.
Through the Pioneer Mountains, Big Sky
Debra, Steve, Whitney, the covered tandem
Only six days in, I think I'll make it.
At the beautiful campsite, I'll rest.

> *"Every time I see an adult on a bicycle, I no longer despair for the future of the human race."* —H.G. Wells

POEM 7: 7 JUNE 2022
Dillon to Alder, Montana

We are cycling most days, traveling east.
We just ride, under the Big Sky to Alder
We rise from the campsite and begin cycling
Gorgeous day, windy, yes, but we're cycling
From Dillon to Alder, all sturdy friends
Rusti, Deb, and Steve cycle as a team
Lewis & Clark traveled across these parts
Naturally sustained productivity,
The historical marker database
The Wortman Ranch sustained health of the land
Sandy, Montana created mountains
We rested and saw the vegetation
Evolved over thousands of years
Imagine, Lewis, Clark, Sacagawea
Rusti, our intrepid dog, like Seaman
Forged on through, as we do, cycling
With the major trucks, we cycled in line
Fifteen miles we cycle, straight ahead now
Focused, clear, straight ahead, Lewis & Clark
Six of us in Sheridan stopped for lunch
Then we rode on for the campsite
"Couldn't be better than this," says Helen.

> "When the spirits are low, when the day appears dark, when work becomes monotonous, when hope hardly seems worth having, just mount a bicycle and go out for a spin down the road, without thought of anything but the ride you are taking." —Arthur Conan Doyle

POEM 8: 8 JUNE 2022
Alder to Ennis

Alder to Ennis, 10 of us, let's ride
Only 29 miles, are you kidding me?
Montana's big sky, a towering dome
Alex's drone soars above, recording
Cycling, of course, cloudy, with nine cyclists
Arrived at Nevada City, for a rest
The Molinari Barrel Piano,
Street piano used by organ grinders
Days of yore, smoking, bar fighting- who knows?
Across the pleasant grass, I see the jail
Sun River Jail, barber shop, western town
We cycle forward, climbing steep, steep hills
Uphill, three miles, I'm exhausted, again
"Suck it up, only 89 days to go!"
George was terrific again, thank you.
Bundled in a winter coat; it's so cold!
Another campsite, a lovely dinner
After Ennis, on to Yellowstone.

> *"The pain you feel today will be the strength you feel tomorrow."* —Chris Foome

POEM 9: 9 JUNE 2022
Earthquake Lake

Cycling, always cycling 71 miles.
A host of 12 focused riders sets out.
Magnificent day, the big sky above
Cameron, Montana, a splendid day
I'm struggling on the hills, feeling the pain
 Pain today will strengthen me for tomorrow
The eyesight of the Hebgen Lake Earthquake
Ghosts of the past linger on Hebgen Lake:
7.2 magnitude forced a landslide
28 fatalities, crushed mountains
Dammed the flow of the Madison River,
Creating Earthquake Lake: calm and pristine
Significant effects of the earthquake,
Strongest and deadliest of the time
Now today, a lake in transition
Quiet, beautiful, museum and lunch
Enjoyed the views and cycled on to West Yellowstone
Exhausted and ready for a restful night.

> *"Get a bicycle. You will not regret it, if you live."*
> —Mark Twain

POEM 10: 10 JUNE 2022
A rest day in Idaho

A day off, the campsite, dusted with snow.
It is spring, but in Idaho, there's snow.
We rest, sleep, so fully, so contently,
How much I needed a rest, finally
I arose, early, doing my laundry
Cycling sheets, whirling around, a rest.
Whites, reds, greens, fleeces, winter coats, swirling
From the cabin, I see a resplendent beef cow,
Framed and ready, as "a bear" I could see
Such a nice place, not cycling, just resting.
Helen, smiling, creates a hot dinner,
And with Alta, Wyoming, Yellowstone,
Yellowstone National Park, please park here!
Mesmerizing puffy white clouds gliding
Reflected in the river down below,
The eyes watching us, either rain or snow
I drive with Helen, I'm just so happy!
Rivers, streams, and lakes, native cutthroat trout!
I cannot believe this, Yellowstone Park!
Look, a chromatic bison, no, for real!
Bisons along the rivers, streams, and lakes!
Snap! Photo over a few feet of grass
Buffalo, bison, bison, buffalo
There, a true bison behind the car, snap!
At 8 o'clock Helen sees the bright bus!
We walk through mire, through muck, to a desert
Under the startling sun, we see geysers
Danger, the incredible geysers!

From the boardwalk, see the hot spring geyser
That is the beautiful sun, Yellowstone!
Grand Prismatic spring creates a rainbow
9:00, Old Faithful faithfully sprays
It's stunning, mesmerizing, perfect.
I'm tired, exhausted, but it's perfect
A few minutes, I gleefully smile
Helen urged this day, and this one was magic!
I will sleep- tomorrow, 57 miles.

> *"Riding a bike is like an Endless Sunday afternoon."*
> —Jens Voigt

POEM 11: 11 JUNE 2022
One Full Week, Yellowstone to Aston, ID

Wow, one full week, can you believe it?
Each day, 66 miles, 71 miles.
Just cycling, all day, every day, it's cold
Yellowstone behind me, Ashton ahead
57 miles, 43 percent
An upgrade, rainy, running up that hill
Yes, West Yellowstone, leaving Montana
Montana, Wyoming, now, Idaho!
Pedaling uphill, huge truckers pass me
Dirt, stones, pebbles, steps, trudging uphill
Cold, it's hard, a long way from Rhode Island
Blinking from the flashing headlights,
Peppered by multitudes of welcome
A sliver of Idaho, cycling
Whitney, cycled on the grainy terrain,
One full week, cycling, oh, a flat tire!
A virgin flat tire strikes in Island Park.
Steve, my hero, pumped the tire, it rained.
Under the magnificent clouds, let's go.
Steve kindly massaged Debra: we're ready.

Each break, with a delicious lunch, we rest.
Crackers, mints, peanut butter and jelly.
Listening to the lake and moving trucks
Every day's tough, 6 degrees, uphill wind
Everyone's tired, endless Sunday it seems:
It was exhausting, but I had my friends
We sat down to a delightful meal
We say to each other, "Look at that view!"
Shadows lengthen as the sun sets above.

"You don't fall off unless you stop pedaling" —Chris Hoy

POEM 12: 12 JUNE 2022
Ashton to Victor, Idaho

Arlen Hall, from Bike Eternity, says,
"You'll find anyone as long as you're kind,"
Cycling across, and worrying there, now.
Idaho, long, sliver, supremacy:
Idaho, thoughts of a dark history
I'll cycle, head down, and pray fervently
Cycling in the wet rain, I cycled—down!
Emily, smiling in the rain, cycled
Alex, on an off day, driving the van
In Tetonia, Deb, Steve, Whitney rode.
Through puddles with Rusti carried behind.
It's nice out there, raining, of course, heads up
Photographs with Sandra, smiling, laughing
Idaho, raining, distance, Grand Tetons
Cycling an alpaca, smiling with Em!
We rested, a break, a lucullan lunch
With Victor, on a bicycle path
Emily and I videotaped it
Lots of laughing and raining in Idaho,
Yes, through kindness, Steve, Deb, Em, and Whitney,
We paused overcast of Idaho
Victor Emporium, Idaho, store,
It rained, and I like the kind people
Pleasant greetings to us through Idaho,
In spite of fears of white supremacy
Traveled through the rain buoyed by kindness

"Age and treachery will overcome youth and skill."
—Fausto Coppi

POEM 13: 13 JUNE 2022
A Storm Coming

Storm coming, snow, rain, 28 degrees,
I relaxed all day, Jackson, Wyoming
A mahogany palace, our brief home
Like Tillie Olsen, had to do laundry
Whites, reds, splendid blue, fleeces, coats, swirling
Peaceful and calm, like a day at my home
Outside, patio dining set, I rest
We gathered in the dining room to eat
Pad Thai, tofu, noodles, chicken, yummy!
But, repacking my bags, and wondering
What's ahead- 31 wintry degrees
With warm gloves, extra clothing, under fleece
I'll enjoy my last supper and prepare
87 days with kind, gentle, friends
420 miles so far; I got this.

> *"A bicycle ride around the world begins with a single stroke."*
> —Scott Stoll

POEM 14: 14 JUNE 2022
28 miles uphill

31 degrees, wintry, snow, gloves, hat,
My goodness, it's freezing, but I'll do it!
Every layer of warmth encloses me
I cycle ahead and ask a stranger,
"Which way, sir?" proffers the anxious cyclist.
"Where are you going?" queried the sage man.
"Revere, Massachusetts. Can I go now?"
He laughs at me: "Revere, go straight ahead!"
Churning, yearning, slowly, I cycle now,
It's Flag Day, it's cold, and I'm exhausted
"Michael, you don't have to do this, slow down."
It's cold, it's slightly raining; I'll do it.
Excelsior, higher, ever upward
I keep going, "This is for you, Debra,"
I pause, panting, Sandra smiles, "Keep going!"
I climb 28 miles, I am exhausted.
I travel upwards to a sign, "Howdy Stranger"
Then I look ahead, it's all downhill now!
30 miles, traveling fast, this is awesome!
In quietude, I feel ataraxy,
Aplomb, composure, yes, tranquility,
Whizzing towards the Great Grand Tetons, I feel good.

POEM 15: 15 JUNE 2022
Grand Tetons

Then, wow, Grand Teton National Park!
Alex, Steve, Debra, and Whitney, cycled
Jackson, Grand Teton National Park!
63 miles, gorgeous, sunny, perfect!
I took over 20 pictures, stunning!
Grand Tetons surround, the world awakens
From every direction, and it's stunning
Cycling behind Steve and Debra, I crunched
Along 15 miles towards the mountains!
Cycling, Wyoming, it's so beautiful
On the dirt path, cycling, a quiet rest
As we stopped to camp, we saw ancient trails
A tremendous day, cycling: now we rest

> *"You are one ride away from a good mood."*
> —Sarah Bentley

POEM 16: 16 JUNE 2022
Odyssey

31 degrees, absolutely cold,
Gloves, again, cycling, upwards to Dubois
It's Bloomsday, Joyce's muse Nora Barnacle,
James Joyce's epic novel of one day,
Cycling America- my odyssey
Today, it's cold, and I am exhausted
42 miles, should be easy, but cold
3,200 feet, sigh, striving up
Sunny, beautiful, we're climbing, uphill
17.25 miles uphill, cycling
It gets warmer, climbing uphill, cycling
Struggling uphill, construction site, go,
Suddenly, the Continental Divide,
9,584 feet
Continental Divide Trail, Wyoming
Separates South Pass, Great Divide Basin
I'm exhausted, take a picture, please!
Roads are so clean, well-kept, perfect riding!
Of course, the snow is still there, it is spring!
Whitney takes a picture, we ride down
Whitney, my partner, enjoys the warm sun
Bloomsday, odyssey, keep moving forward.

POEM 17: 17 JUNE 2022.
Wyoming Winds

Oh, my, Zephyrus will blow us anew
A snowy range of mountains always there,
The winds blow over 70 miles now!
Just cycling, slugging against this hard wind.
Blowing winter snows, leaving ridge, slopes bare,
Exposing grasses, shrubs along the side
Elk, deer, antelope somehow overcome
These harsh winter conditions, somehow live.
Inspired, I grit my teeth, and want to win
Sandra and Whitney, ugh, exhausted, done
Discouraged, but in Lander- a nice night
All together, laughing, smiling, so sweet.
Just six of us, a little smaller now
Whitney, Steve, Emily, Alex, Debra,
Ice cream, yes, "World famous, chokecherry shakes!"
Delightful night, we rest, until the winds
Sandra yells, "Michael, the winds, get out now!"
I crumple the tents, and move to safety
Wyoming Winds, seeming winds in the spring
Each day, the winds exhaust me; I'll make it.

> *"I'm so tired/ I don't know what to do/ I'm so tired/ My mind is set on you/ I wonder should I call you/ But i know what would do."*
> —John Lennon, Paul McCartney, The Beatles

POEM 18: 18 JUNE 2022
I'm so tired

Yes, Lander, Wyoming, I'm so tired
With a plan for 70 miles, I can't
You go, Steve and Debra, I'll take a break
Over 700 miles, 18 days,
Yes, I'm so tired, and I'll just relax
Listen to my body and gather strength
"Come to me, you who are weary, burdened,
Take my yoke upon you and learn from me."
Sandra, Alex, Steve and Debra cycled
58 miles, it was windy as hell
Yes, Montana, Idaho, Wyoming
But I will persevere, I'll do this.
Already, I've seen this, simply magic,
But, I will ride soon, from Jeffrey City
Desolate remote town with one motel
Green Mountain Motel, 58 persons
A desert-like motel with kind people
With the sun setting, it's spectacular!
With perseverance, determination,
I will cycle, no matter what now!

> "Juneteenth has never been a celebration of victory, or an acceptance of the way things are. Instead, it's a celebration of progress. It's an affirmation that despite the most painful parts of our history, things do get better. America can change." —President Barack Obama

POEM 19: 19 JUNE 2022
Juneteeth

In Jeffery City, Wyoming, let's ride
Alex, Whitney, Steve, Debra we will ride
Happy Father's Day messages arrive
Jackson, Liza, Zachary, Carolyn
Send videos from home, I hear smiling
Sending encouragement and love to me
From far away, my family glowed.
And, of course, Juneteenth, a celebration
President Obama said, "It's progress,"
Progress through the painful parts, challenges
That way growth lies, ahead through the struggle
I'll cycle the mountains ahead of me
In Rawlins, alone, uphill, keep going:
Lost, of course, my iPhone charged, damnit!
"Excuse me, will you charge my iPhone, please, sir?"
He kindly charged it, and directed me.
Another KOA campsite, thank you
"Things get better. America can change."

> *"If anything is endemic to Wyoming it is wind. This big room is swept out daily, leaving a bone yard of fossils, agates, and carcasses in every stage of decay. Though it was water that initially shaped the state, wind is the meticulous gardener, raising dust and pruning the sage."*
> —Gretel Ehrlich

POEM 20: 20 JUNE 2022
Rawlins, Wyoming

Union General John Aaron Rawlins
Fought the civil war for America
Ulysses Grant was a great president,
But he died from tuberculosis,
Another great man fighting for us.
Another day, another laundry run
Whites, reds, greens, splendid blues, shirts, coats, swirling
Folding the laundry, quietly listening
Walking past the store, heading back to camp
Suddenly, a maelstrom, fifteen minutes
Rain, winds, Wyoming winds, destroyed our tents
I videotaped my tent, swirling tents
Dèjá vu all over again, right?
Then, it was beautiful sight, clear, sunny,
Half the tents were repacked, dinner was made
Together now, we laughed with each other.

POEM 21: 21 JUNE 2022
Interstate 80

Happy Birthday, Debra, I love you, friend,
61 miles, Rawlins to Riverside
Cycling, a new day, prepared and ready
We leave Rawlins on Interstate 80
Five of us focused on the highway
Only "15 miles," I could see Jersey!
Such a calm ride, but, of course, I'm anxious!
Brief rest stop in Saratoga, and then
The road slightly inclines, rest for a lunch
Sunny, breezy cycle to Riverside
Jeffrey City, Wyoming, bit bigger
7,142 feet
The elevation of Jeffrey City!
Riverside, only 59 people!
Yes, we celebrated Debra's birthday,
Dancing and singing with these friends of mine
Rusti, Steve, and Debra hugged closely now,
In Ecclesiastes, we have a number:
They have a good return in their labor:
Laboring, each day, we've each one of us
We are together so close, with long miles
Behind and many miles to go ahead.

> *"So do fear, for I am with you; do not be dismayed, for I am your God. I will strengthen you and help you; I will uphold you with my righteous hand."* —Isaiah 41:10

POEM 22: 21 JUNE 2022 (2)
A Fall

Cycling together binds us together.
Wyoming, each day turns a wintry wind
Cycling, sunny, Deb, Steve, Whitney, Alex
Cycling, beautiful day, but I'm struggling
Each person, fading away, passes me
Suddenly, I slip, falling to the ground
"Whitney, Steve, Deb, Alex can you help me?"
I struggled, but two kind, gentle women
Stopped and asked me, "can we give you some help?"
They kindly drove me and my bike four miles
Air conditioned comfort, restful truck ride.
Sandra was so happy to hear us
Gently and easily, I rode on with them.
"For I'm with you; do not be dismayed
Christ says, "I will strengthen you and help you."
We cycled, together, Wyoming, sigh
"Obligamus nos," yes, kindness binds us

POEM 23: 22 JUNE 2022

That fought with us upon Saint Crispin's day
"Riverside to Walden, Colorado"

It is a perfect day, day 35
Goodbye, Wyoming, Hi, Colorado
Whitney, Alex, Steve, Deb, 49 miles
With some rough construction, we cycled past
To the encampment, cycling aways, go!
Welcome to Colorful Colorado!
Bye, Montana, Idaho, Wyoming!
Now with 5 states, we have Colorado!
Take a picture, please, it's beautiful
Cycling, incline, of course, always, always
With a multitude swarm of mosquitoes
We rest in a cozy motel for night
In the singular home, we gathered home
"He that outlives that day, come safely home"
You do not know what's ahead, so rest up.

POEM 24: 23 JUNE 2022
"Cameron Pass, 10,276 feet"

Cameron Pass, a Northern mountain pass
Larimer County, Colorado
10,276 feet
Visitors, everywhere, maybe we drive
Not me, I'll cycle, I plan to ride up
 72 miles today, we'll make it;
We're cycling, 6 of us, 20 miles, nice
The first miles were easy and exquisite
Previously, Sandra foretold the pass
Don't talk about it, yes, hear no evil!
We love this path, 20 miles, I like it!
The water break is great, for one last rest.
Then Whitney and I were struggling uphill
 8 miles, uphill, "Whitney, let's take a rest"
"No, keep going, friend, you got this, Michael!"
Steep, steep, uphill, I'm grumbling at Whitney
"Please, Whitney, let us stop," panting, panting
Through the State Forest State Park, I'm struggling
 Bright fluorescent orange signs: "Road work ahead"
What a spectacular, beautiful, view!
Climbing uphill, Radiohead, James Brown
"Say it loud, I'm Black and I'm proud!": push, push.
Whitney stops to rest, and I go, cycling,
Struggling, I was in pain, panting, wheezing
I've got to finish now, I reach inside
At the top of the pass Steve and Debra
Celebrated my arrival, made it!
Me, I was exhausted, I met Steve first:
"Steve, I can't do this, I'm done, I'm finished"

But Steve, determined, "Congratulations!"
"You went uphill, and now you go downhill!"
We took photos and mounted our bikes.
Then, with the music I went, fast, downhill
15 miles, wow! 40 miles per hour!
With my hands gripping, exhilarated
I finally stopped, I was so excited!
Cycling, happy, to Stove Prairie Landing
Photos with the documentarists who
Later told us they thought, "They won't make it!
We walked through Cache la Poudre River
Bathing our souls, after 72 miles
Alex, Emily, Debra, the river
The cool water, bubbling, rewarding us.
Yes, with our family, I laugh, rested.

> *"So, live. Live. Fight like hell. And when you get too tired to fight then lay down and rest and let somebody else fight for you."* —Stuart Scott

POEM 25: 24 JUNE 2022
Boulder, Colorado

71-mile day, maybe lost again
Cycling, beautiful, oh my, I fell down!
The first time, no matter, 3,000 miles
The mountains hold a magnificent view
From Bellevue by the lovely, cooling stream.
In Loveland, a break, and chatter talking
Our first event in Boulder, Steve's worried.
It's a sunny day, but Steve strokes onward
I couldn't make it, but I could relax
I cycle, with Whitney, 10 miles to Boulder
Now, a celebration, Sari, Charlie
Friends from Pepper Pike, Ohio- my past!
I'll sleep for three nights, this is magical!
Sari's so wonderful, welcoming me.
Boulder's an unusual place,
With a deer, climbing upwards, I'm happy
Dinner with Sari, Charlie with the dog.
A place of comfort, of home, I'm pleased now.

POEM 26: 25 JUNE 2022
A Haven in Boulder, Colorado

With green peppers, chicken, and a salad,
A marvelous dinner on the lit porch!
This is dinner with Sari and Charlie!
Yes, The Weinbergers know how to treat me!
They have a luxurious massage chair!
Sari drives me down the steep hill to meet
My nephew Zander, who lives in Boulder.
With my bearded face and Midd polo shirt
I smile at the cameras, no cycling!
Busy Boulder, fascinating people!
Troubadours on flute, the jugglers abound
George Lundeen, Sorrel Sky, Hearts on a swing
This is magical, yes, Colorado!
I see everything, and I share Shakespeare:
"Speak the speech, I pray you, as I pronounced it to
you, trippingly on the tongue.
But if you mouth it, as many of our players do,
I had as lief the town crier spoke my lines"
With my aphasia, Shakespeare speaks for me.

POEM 27: 26 JUNE 2022
Stroke Onward Event, Sterne Park

I feel comfortable, now, yes, Stroke Onward
An event, we tell our stories to all
Stroke survivors, care partners, SLP's
A community of love and support.
Books: "Identity Theft", "Finding My Words"
 Leora and Richard are there for me.
Perfectly shy, but they're my family,
"You are awesome, we are so proud of you."
Half-brother hugged me, her wife, Leora
Even here, surround us, Job 42:10:
"The Lord restored his fortunes and gave him"
I feel so heartwarmed, so beloved, friends,
Spending time with my long distance cousins.
Debra speaks about her moving journey,
Then, I too, speak, share my story with all.
I love this space, speaking of aphasia
In Cameron pass, I was climbing, but now,
Three days later, I'm speaking, beautiful!
We hug goodbye, and cycle for our camp.
Next, a 37-mile day ahead.

POEM 28: 27 JUNE 2002
Boulder to Boyd Lake State Park

With gentlest way to Colorado
Sandra videotaped the sunny day
Cycling, 37-miles, no mountains!
We're cycling, Whitney, Steve and Emily
Rusti the dog in his mobile home
With such a ride, my, what a sunny day,
Yes, we camped and dined in Boyd Lake State Park
What a gorgeous day, as the sunsets east

POEM 29: 28 JUNE 2022
Briggsdale, Colorado

Each day, we're cycling, yes, on a mission
We're cycling, and we can kind of groove now
Another gorgeous day, Arlen cycles
Smooth paths, Windsor, at one with my bike
This ride is fantastic, smooth ride, easy!
Sandra, videotaped me, music blasting!
In Greeley, Colorado, we cycle
Can you believe it, yes, 63 miles!
We gather, together, only six friends
Crow Valley Recreation area
It's too darn hot: Em drapes her handkerchief.
Setting up the tent is too much for me
I'll sleep, right there, in the clear, open air
A calm night, I lay me down to sleep

POEM 30: 29 JUNE 2022
Briggsdale to Sterling 58 Miles

New Raymer to Sterling, Colorado
8 miles New Raymer, then 43 miles,
Alex, Whitney, Sandra and I forge on
8:11am, Briggsdale, it's too darn hot
At 1:00, Whitney takes a photo
While cycling, a picture, it's a perfect shot!
The orange Ariat, Stroke Onward, zips down
I keep cycling, spring's turned to summer
Colorado started out hard, but now
Fewer than 29 days, spring's turned to summer
Once in the high mountains; now, beautiful
Smooth roads unfurl with mountains in our past
Cyclists see more of this beautiful world.

> *"Cyclists see considerably more of this beautiful world than any other class of citizens."* —Dr. K.K. Doty

POEM 31: 30 JUNE 2022
Sterling, Colorado, Zero miles

There's a map on the van where we keep track
 Astoria, Oregon to Sterling
The trail of black marker growing longer
Elevation, almost 4,000 feet
Laundry for us, and bath day for Rusti
Debra, Whitney, Alex, were surprised too!
Another calm day on our trek forward.

> *"What a computer is to me is it's the most remarkable tool that we've ever come up with, and it's the equivalent of a bicycle for our minds."* —Steve Jobs

POEM 32: 1 JULY 2022 (1)
The Good Samaritan

You, friend, love the Lord God with all your heart,
Yes, and with your soul and with all your strength
With all your mind; love your neighbor as you!
The hot sun blazes, flattens my tire
I sit there, deflated like my tire
Perplexed, what to do, how do I fix it?
Like the two "weak" women, feeling helpless
But then, the Good Samaritan arrived:
Effortlessly changing the flat quickly,
Smoothly; he's a bicycle mechanic:
Answer to the question, "Who's my neighbor?"
From Jerusalem to Jericho
A small town, the last in Colorado
He filled the now plump black tire, easily,
What wondrous beauty, so magnificent!
Manna in the way of starving people.

> "Marriage is a wonderful invention; but then again, so is bicycle repair kit." —Billy Connolly

POEM 33 1 JULY 2022 (2)
Sterling, Colorado to Holyoke, Colorado

Sterling, Holyoke, 40 miles, campsite
Hot day, with a bit of tragedy:
Steve, Debra, while cycling, Rusti fell out
Panicked, Steve, Debra, rushed to hospital:
All's well, but he had a rough road, Rusti
Cycling, always, we rode, cycled always
Thank goodness for the Good Samaritan
Busy day cycling, but, of course, onward.

POEM 34: 2 JULY 2022
Holyoke, Colorado to Imperial, Nebraska

I'm telling you, riding a bicycle's fun!
This cycling, with fewer people, rides
It's Saturday morning, 45 miles
Imperial, Nebraska, new state!
It's amazing, zero percent humid
Just cycling, from Holyoke to Lamar
Nebraska, with the motto, "The Good Life"
We stayed in a motel, yes, laundry day
We made a delicious feast for dinner
Red cabbage, lettuce, cheese, tortellini
We met with a fellow traveling man
Cycling retrograde, from West to the East
Whitney, Arlen, Alex, Em, Steve, Deb
Beautiful day, Nebraska, the good life

> *"The bicycle is a curious vehicle. Its passenger is its engine."*
> —John Howard

POEM 35: SUNDAY, 3 JULY 2022
Imperial, Nebraska to McCook, Nebraska

It's 95 degrees, and we enter
Wauneta, entering Central Time Zone
Cycling, forward through heat, but clouds ahead
At the campsite, the rain pours down on us.
"Let's dance, put on your red shoes, dance the blues"
Em, Alex are laughing, raining, dancing
McCook, Nebraska, the rain never stops
A sleeping bag, a pillow, a good night
Suddenly, fireworks for 10 minutes
Oh, Lord, it is late, please, let me sleep, please.
Silently sleeping, the contours of life.

> *"As a kid I had a dream—I wanted to own my own bicycle. When I got the bike I must have been the happiest boy in Liverpool, maybe the world. I lived for that bike. Most kids left their bike in the backyard at night. Not me. I insisted on taking mine indoors and the first night I even kept it in my bed."* —John Lennon, The Beatles

POEM 36: 4 JULY 2022
75 miles McCook to Alma, Nebraska
Independence Day

Fireworks celebrations surround us all
75 McCook to Alma, Nebraska
Independence Day, the Fourth of July
Blasting fireworks, annoying, bang, bang!
It's 7:19am, and Sandra's ready
We videotape, 104 degrees
We are ready, blinking lights, let's ride, friends
I'm cycling behind Sandra, what is that?
Hell in a bucket, damnit, flat tire!
Sandra kindly fixed my tire, thank you
My speaker fell off of my handlebars.
In Oxford, Nebraska, it is hot, friends
Alex, BAM, another flat tire, shoot!
Hot, 104 degrees, already.
Steve stops with Alex, yet another flat
Then we rest after 75 miles
America's birthday from the heartland.

POEM 37: 5 JULY 2022
Through hardship to the stars
Alma, Nebraska to Smith Center, Kansas

Cycling east, through town populations of
Only 134 persons
Waved goodbye to Nebraska, "The Good life"
Franklin, Nebraska, Sandra videotaped
Kansas, "Ad astra Per Aspera"
From the Latin, "Through hardships to the stars"
Oh, Kansas, warning of hardships ahead.
I didn't know what that meant was to come.
I looked back, and I waved to Nebraska
Whole time, I was rolling up and down hills
It was good to cycle east, on, Kansas!
Another night, another campsite,
Arlen met the mayor of the small town.
I rested, and I looked for a tree:
There must be a tree somewhere in Kansas.
Arlen arrived and fixed our tires!
I slept inside RV due to hail storms
Through hardships to the stars, turn the page, please.

POEM 38: 6 JULY 2022
"Bellevue, Kansas, it's Hot"

One month ago, 'twas 31 degrees
Now, Kansas, hot, 104 degrees
We're cycling and then, Whitney had to stop:
Ah, Kansas, Historical Marker
Lebanon, geographical center
1630 miles, both ways
To Boston, Mass and to San Francisco,
We're delicately, tenuously
Equally far from cities east and west
In between San Francisco and Boston
In a park, three miles north and one mile west
Is the exact geographic center
Of the 48 contiguous states
Well, of course, Alaska and Hawaii
The location is officially marked
They say Dodge City, but it's very close
Alex, Whitney photographed selfie
Even Emily, Alex, Whitney, too!
Across the way, Kansas, so cool, so nice
We're half way there, living on a prayer!
We cycled from Mankato to Kansas
The heat is savage, 98 degrees
It's hot, we stop, 104 degrees
Dallas, Arlen's son, Emily, Alex
Of course, Steve and Debra are cycling.

64 miles, 104 degrees
Whitney, Sandra, Steve, Deb, Dallas, enjoy
But, celebration, Emily, Alex
In Belleville, Mexican restaurant
Melancholy is incompatible.

> *"Melancholy is incompatible with bicycling."*
> —James E. Starrs

POEM 39: 7 JULY 2022
Nothing today, Laundry Day

No cycling, 50th day for Steve, Debra
From Astoria, to Belleville, Kansas
Laundry, again, whites, reds, blues, orange, again
Another calming day, reading essays,
Steve, Debra, Alex, Whitney, Emily
Take a private room, very posh, so nice
Half way there, 50 down, 50 to go
"Thank God for my inimitable soul"

> *"Think of bicycles as rideable art that can just about save the world."* —Grant Petersen

POEM 40: 8 JULY 2022
Belleville, Kansas to Marysville, Kansas

Belleville, Kansas, 64 miles, it's hot
Whitney, Alex, Dallas, will travel, hot
It's only 7:33am,
But, we cycle, bam, I lose my speaker,
Into Salt Creek, damnit, into the drink
Yes, pumping my legs, and gritting our teeth
Once, in Kansas, I saw the angry dog
Everything, it seems in Kansas, ugh!
A copse barely the land, where is the trees?
In Haddam, we cycle, seeing the land,
In Hanover, Alex rides down hill
At lunch everyone had a rest, smoothly
It was beautiful, cycling iPhone tunes
We stopped by Marysville, only 10 miles
Then, it was mud, gravel, absolute sludge
We trudged, slowly, the soil, the silt, dirt
The hard clay was cracked and I tentatively,
Seething, "ad astra per aspera"
Finally, we stopped, washed our bicycles
Arlen, Steve, Debra, and my hosed our wheels
"Searing our lungs as though we're being chased"
Kansas, windstorms, winds, heat, and searing days

> "Think of the hopes, the dreams, the brilliance, the pure force of will that, over the eons, has gone into the creation of the Cadillac de Ville. Bicycle riders would have us throw all this on the ash heap of history." —P.J. O'Rourke

POEM 41: 9 JULY 2022
The Crash

69 miles, long, arduous, Kansas,
It's been five days and I am exhausted
Hot weather, thunderstorms, torrential rain
Unbelievable, dogs running through sludge
No trees, I long for green shadows of shade
We cycle with Emily and Whitney
"It's a great day and beautiful weather,"
Riding each day, Em and Alex are great!
We cycled, playing iTunes, just cycling
The sun, the wind, it's all good cycling
38 miles, Whitney, Emily slowed down
Cautious, then – BAM, over the handlebars!
I hit the edge of a culvert and flew
Arlen lifted my bike, and said, "we're done!"
"But, why, I'm going to Horton, let's go!"
He showed me a photo of my black eye
Quickly swollen, Shawn got me in the van
She drove me to doctors, no one's there, damn!
A friendly doctor then opened the door.
She kindly—and quickly— did the x-ray
In a neck brace, eyes swollen, black and blue
After a few hours, I was napping
A broken eye bone and a concussion
Back at the camp, Horton, Kansas, I slept
Crashing is part of cycling oh, screw you!
Kansas, "Ad astra per aspera"
Hardship happened, when will the stars arrive?

> *"Crashing is part of cycling as crying is part of love."*
> —Johan Museeuw

POEM 42: 10 JULY 2022
Goodbye, Sandra

Is it true, are you leaving from Horton?
Yes, it's true, I'm leaving on a jet plane
Or bicycling across New Mexico
Has it truly been only one brief month?
Montana, Wyoming, Colorado,
Idaho: with patience and clarity
I remember: "Michael, take it easy."
"Take your time, cycling, use your mind, each day"
We camped outdoors, Nebraska, Kansas
6 states, 1,406
Give or take a few miles, but you're leaving
Sadness, anxiety, and gratitude
You're a warrior, pick up your sword, fight!
I'll miss you; it's so hard to say goodbye.

> *"You're a warrior, warriors don't give up and they don't back down. Pick up your sword and fight."* —Anonymous

POEM 43: 10 JULY 2022 (1)
Kansas, The Sunflower State

Charybdis, Ancient Greek, a sea monster,
She, with the sea Monster, Scylla, just fought
Odysseus and Jason fought them too:
Ah, Kansas, "Carry on my wayward son,"
A rolling majestic, crumpling hot road,
With a sun of 104 degrees
Heat advisory, again, over hills
And at night, there's a tornado siren:
Kansas, heat winds, 60 miles per hour
Yes, Stroke Across America, cycling,
It was hard, sometimes crushing, flat tires,
The wind, the blowing wind, destroying dreams
Kansas, only 4,041ft:
Only the copse trees remain hot weather
Charydis and Scylla fought the great seas,
But Kansas, cycling through mud, sweat, and tears.
Until the unexpected crash happens
But cycling supports me, gives me succor
While cycling, I'm a living miracle.
I wonder about Charybdis and Scylla,
I can fight these monsters, but I just don't care
St. Theresa of Avila opines,
"To have courage for whatever comes in life
Everything lies in that." That is something.
As we continue, cycling to win—now
Practice, patience, prayer, that's all we can do.

POEM 44: 10 JULY 2022 (2)
Time passes in Kansas

Thank you for your care, Shawn, moving along.
Yeah, I'm stuck, been sleeping in the RV,
Recovering but restless, no biking.
Moving through Kansas, the Sunflower State.
We rest in Lancaster, Kansas, no trees
Then Rushville, Missouri, so long, Kansas!
Picture with Dallas, UGH, my eyes are shut!
We see Alex and Dallas smiling, too
Missouri, the Show Me State, is next.
We stop, Weston, 52 miles, we camped
Dinner with Sarah Srock, a friend from home
What a beautiful evening together!
We wave goodbye, and I rest in RV
Thinking of wellness and recovery
Ready to be back on my bicycle.

POEM 45: 11 JULY 2022
I'll be back

That culvert, you've got to be kidding me
Fewer than two days, I seethe, a culvert
"If he do not, tis no matter there"
In the car, I go to a posh hotel
A pharmacy for a razor and cream
Scrape, scrape, scrape, sigh; it does not come off!
Wild hair, wild beard, sigh, still a mountain man
We meet Jackie, she's from New Mexico!
We have a lunch with air conditioning
Black American Aphasia Group Zoom!
We talk, we laugh; "Damn, what's with the black eye?"
Smiling, "I've a concussion, I'll be back!"
Return of the Jedi, only 3 days!
I may not be cycling, but still working
Tomorrow, I hope, Shawn will cut this beard
Next: Kansas City for a baseball game!
The Royals versus the Detroit Tigers
Dallas, Whitney, Alex, Emily, me
Four more stadiums, make a note of it!
I just love it, I love it, let's go:
I care about this damn Kansas City!

POEM 46: 12 JULY 2022
"Kansas City to KMBC, Kansas, an Event"

Lights, camera, action! An event - yes!
First, of course, Shawn will take a full clipping
It will be my first shave in a month- sharp!
Now you see the beard, now you don't, super!
We lull around, yes, laundry, whites, blues, reds
I speak with journalist Ed Fitzpatrick
The Boston Globe will record the journey
Yes, I'm so inspired, I'm so humbled!
WMBC arrives, speaks with Steve
Each step, patiently, cycling, together
At the event, Debra speaks, Whitney speaks,
And I speak, telling my story anew
Deb, you did superb in Colorado
Seems like ages, but Deb and Steve, thank you
The secret success is daily routine

> *"I'm from Kansas City, Missouri. No one has to give a damn about my story."* —Tech N9ne

POEM 47: 13 JULY 2022
Comeback

"Don't call it comeback, I been here for years"
That's right, 3 days, a concussion, I'm back!
A 66-mile day ahead; well, let's go!
Whitney, Jackie, a newcomer, Molly
Whitney's sharp parents from California
Alex, and of course Steve and Deb, cycling
It's a gorgeous day, cycling, beautiful!
Katy Trail State Park, a flat, crushed limestone
For perfect cycling across this nation
240 miles, a shady path.
After 20 miles, I rest, I feel good
Arlen slows down and we enjoy a lunch
Arlen says, "Are you ready for 19 miles?"
Don't call it a comeback, I've been here for years!
Fight, fight like hell, keep living, survivor!
With Alex, I cycle, and, yes, a flat
We cycle, 38 miles, and I felt good,
Debra videotaped, and it was humid
Arrived in Windsor, 95 degrees
Warm, humid, campsite, we're living the life!

"If you get tired, learn to rest, not quit!" —Banksy

POEM 48: 14 JULY 2022
From Windsor to Boonville, 60 miles

"Wouldn't it be nice if we were older?
Then we wouldn't have to wait so long
And wouldn't it be nice to live together
In the kind of world where we belong?"
Traveling 60 miles, singing Beach Boys
Emily is great, she's so positive
From Sedalia, we ride to Pilot Grove

The Missouri Kansas Texas railroad
Emily, laughing of course, smile twinkles
The sunshine is as lovely as the day
Cycling, Molly, Tony, Whitney, Steve, Deb
Oh, yes, Tony, Whitney's father, cycling
To Boonville, cycling, on limestone pebbles.
"And wouldn't it be nice to live together?"

> *"Don't tell people your plans. Show them your results."*
> —Anonymous

POEM 49: 15 JULY 2022
Boonville, to Jefferson City, 59 Miles

Alex's last video for three days.
Heart's broken, but we'll meet in St. Louis
Cycling in New Franklin, with the huge clouds
Alex, naturally, smiles all around
Through a tunnel along the limestone path
Such verdant trees, not like copse in Kansas
Then, yes, Rocheport, the Missouri River
Alex, no matter what, smiling, cycling
Jefferson City, Arlen washed the bikes
Another hotel, I'm living in style!
Shawn, Steve, Molly, Deb, Tony and Whitney
Dallas, Arlen, Jackie, and I enjoy
Wonderful evening with Japanese food
A close bond family together tonight
It is your mind that you have to convince

> *"Your body can stand almost anything. It's your mind that you have to convince."* —Anonymous

POEM 50: 16 JULY 2022
Jefferson City—No Cycling

A short one, for sure, hotel, no cycling
Tony, of course, it's hot, let's go golfing
Over 90 degrees, humid, laundry
Oh, yes, reds, whites, blues, orange, a laundry day
We all gathered for Jefferson City
Domenico Italian Restaurant
I loved Italian pasta lasagna
A new family, Steve, of course, Zoey,
Drew, Molly, Debra, Whitney, Tony, Shawn
Drew, Steve's roommate, Yale University
Zoey, Drew's Daughter from Washington U
Bonded, a few days, with us, Katy Trail
Yes, what a marvelous time, Missouri!
You do not have to climb the whole staircase
You know, people, friends, just take the first step

POEM 51: 17 JULY 2022
Katy Trail State Park, Jefferson to Hermann

59 miles, the Capital, Hermann
A beautiful, humid day, it will rain
Wow, what a magnificent Capital
Cycling, to Missouri River, huge gates
Smiling, always smiling, we skim along
It's easier than cycling up mountains
On the limestone path, Jackie travels forth
Tebbetts, Missouri: population, 64
Through Mokane and Portland, there is mud, yuck.
There's cakes and cakes of it, humid, rainy
The whole Specialized bicycle, mud!
The mud splatters our legs and our helmets.
My back, stained with a full mud triangle
Cycling, we see the Missouri River

60 days behind; only 40 more
Hermann, a German Town, ah, wine country
We have a delicious feast, 9 of us!
Ah, now I can see my dark, dark, tan too!
Wearing my new, dark sunglasses.
Yes, chicken and blueberry cheesecake
39 miles, wow, let's party tonight!
Steve and Molly playing shuffleboard
Molly and Debra laugh and smile as one.
And Tony and Whitney dance, "Take me Home"
What a fabulous night, wine, dancing, beers
39 miles, are you kidding me?
Ernest Hemingway would have enjoyed

> "The bicycle riders drank much wine, and were burned and browned by the sun." —Ernest Hemingway

POEM 52: 18 JULY 2022
"Hermann to Augusta, 39.1 miles"

Another day of beautiful cycling
Molly, Whitney, Drew, Zoey, Tony, Steve,
And Debra, along the Missouri River.
Marthasville, Missouri, Daniel Boone's home

Grandfather to 68 grandchildren.
Picture this one: Molly, Tony, Whitney
Smiling in the sun, California kids
Augusta, Missouri, eight of us beam
There's a picture pointing us to the East
We rest in the nice comfortable bed
Halcyon spa studio bed & breakfast
12 disciples for dinner with Jackie
Nothing compares to the simple pleasures.

"Nothing compares to the simple pleasure of riding a bike."
—President John Kennedy

POEM 53: 19 JULY 2022
Stories of the land
"Augusta to St. Louis, 58 miles"

We eleven joyfully continue,
Steve, Debra videotape us, and we're off!
Cycling, 58 miles, sunny, perfect day
Through St. Charles, Bridgeton, Ferguson
Memories of the Ferguson protests
Michael Brown, 10 August 2014
His killing sparked a vigorous debate
For several days, Ferguson, planned, fought
First wave, Mike Brown, next wave Darren Wilson
Third wave, widespread, rioting, arson.
Now, 8 years on, Ferguson is peaceful
Cycling, uphill, I can picture those days.
Cycling across, up and down, up and down,
—

Stop at North Riverfront Park, Missouri
With views of the mighty Mississippi
My words can't capture the river's grandeur.
Mississippi River- west, Oregon
East, Revere Beach, Massachusetts, I'm home:
 I'm coming, ever nearer, cycling now
Standing at the massive river, visions
Of Lewis & Clark, Samuel Clemens
Huck, Jim, the tarred and feathered duke and king
The novel unfolded on this river.
I can hear my eleventh grade students
Now it's mumbling in my ears- aphasia
The spirit of the stories are strong here
Now, "a dream itself is but a shadow".

Cycling east, now we see the Gateway Arch
This day was a journey through memories
Rural to the city of St. Louis
"The best rides are the ones where you bite off
More than you can chew," yes, "and live through it"

> *"The best rides are the ones where you bite off more than you can chew, and live through it."* —Doug Bradbury

POEM 54: 20 JULY 2022
"The Show Me State"

Missouri, our tenth state, cycling now.
Now, we've traveled through 9 states, yes, 9 states
Cycling against the rain, snow, freezing, heat,
Now, we come to Missouri, The Show Me State!
Katy Trail State Park, yes, 200 miles
Cycling along green, shaded gravel paths.
Climbing, so slightly with a pleasant grain
Sedalia, Mokane, Portland, Marthasville,
Hermann, sweet German, and fine wineries
And Augusta, with cute bed & breakfast.
Katy Trail had Scott Joplin and Daniel Boone
And Lewis & Clark's long expedition
Cycling towards St. Louis from St. Charles, hot!
Beautiful state park meshed with urban feel,
The muddy Missouri, Mississippi
And how I can't wait for the Gateway Arch!
Together, we cycled on, day by day.
Understanding our new identities
As stroke survivors, cyclists, family.
Always cycling against and with ourselves.
We're miles away cycling for ourselves
Two rules; one, never quit; two, never quit

POEM 55: 20 JULY 2022
"An Event in St. Louis, Gateway Arch"

With Washington University,
Dined with Shawn, Jackie, Alex, Emily!
Of course, Arlen, Steve, Deb, Tony, Molly
The documentarists were there, filming
A month ago, they're saying "Can't do it!"
"How you like me know?" friends, cycling, sweating!
On Wednesday, yet another hotel.
The Gateway Arch National Park
Adam Laye, Roxbury Latin alum!
Adam, he's much bigger, distinguished
From George Washington U. to St. Louis
A treasurer now for the mayor, oh, yes!
I feel so proud, and, yes, still, aphasia
I worked so hard to teach, but it's gone now
Ah, aphasia, let it go, let it lie
When I am cycling, I can let it go.
Let it rest: I'm cycling across country!
I walked between Sugarfire Smokehouse
Huge beef steer replica for a statue
98 degrees, in the shade, real hot!
Tower Grove Park, Uber, for the event
Several dozen are in attendance here.
Debra and Steve spoke, so eloquently
Whitney spoke, she felt more comfortable
Honoring Stroke Across America
Such a proud plaque for our proud St. Louis

Flannery O'Neil, a Stroke Survivor,
Smiled beautifully for the cherished plaque
Cycling Missouri, Zoey and Drew
We loved the time in St. Louis so much.

> *"Boys, be ambitious. Be ambitious not for money or for selfish aggrandizement, not for that evanescent thing which men call fame. Be ambitious for the attainment of all that a man ought to be."* —William Clark

POEM 56: 21 JULY 2022
St. Louis, Missouri to Litchfield, Illinois

So long, Missouri, on to Illinois
Goodbye Gateway Arch, fare thee well, river,
Now, get your kicks from the Route 66
Traveling east from Mississippi, Litchfield
Debra and Steve, always cycling tandem
Illinois, Land of Lincoln, cycling east
Route 66, symbolizes romance
Born 1926, freedom alive
We're traveling northeast to Chicago
Jackie Shane smiles, Debra and Steve, always
Whitney waved goodbye, Molly and Tony
Whitney, my cycling partner is ready
Camp Dubois, Illinois, Lewis &Clark
Can you imagine, Lewis & Clark west!
Can you remember in Montana,
Museum in Lolo, yes, Montana
Lewis, Clark, voyage of discovery
"We proceeded on," opined Lewis & Clark
It's really summer, everyday, now.

POEM 57: 22 JULY 2022

I am content

I have small, simple things, yes I'm content
A small dish, quiche with broccoli, and yes,
Zucchini bread: dash of peanut butter.
Doesn't get any better than that.
Cycling, 18 miles today, I'm content
With my wife, I cycle, I imagine:
25 years, married: I do love her.
Through marriage, through children, yes, through a stroke
We strive, tentatively, to make our way.
With Liza, with Jackson, with Zachary,
I love my children and I love my wife.
25 years, William Shakespeare, ah, yes,
He mentions, mulls, "The Merchant of Venice,"
And he thinks Shylock, angry, despondent,
And I hear him, and thinking of Shylock:
" And I am content?" For a moment: YES!
Happy anniversary, Carolyn!

POEM 58: 23 JULY 2022
Springfield to Goodfield, 77 Miles

Steve, Debra, Alex, and Whitney, cycling
62 miles, only 84 feet!
Whitney, Emily Springfield, Lincoln home
But we cycle past, darn it, we're cycling
Yet, another hot day, Route 66
It's hot, easily 95 degrees
We arrive - Mackinaw Valley Vineyard
Rested, Timberline Campground, Illinois
Whitney, Emily, Alex, Deb, Steve, camped
It's a different world, where you come from
Golf carts, swimming pools, deep fried Oreos
It doesn't matter how slow, just go, friend

> *"Illinois surpasses every spot of equal extent upon the face of the globe in fertility of soil in the proportionable amount of the same which is sufficiently level for actual cultivation."*
> —President Abraham Lincoln

POEM 59: 24 JULY 2022
A rainy day in Goodfield, Illinois: Three Songs

"Let it rain, let your love rain down on me"
Plaintive the song, solemnly, by Eric Clapton
Dry, and dusty road, I need to get to my home
Oh, I need to get back home to cool, cool, rain
Blame it on the rain was fallin' fallin'
The stars that didn't shine for us on that night
As it rained, rained, rained, all the lazy day.

> *"There was nowhere to go but everywhere, so just keep on rolling under the stars. Nothing behind me, everything ahead of me, as is ever so on the road."* —Jack Kerouac

poem 60: 25 july 2022
Father-in-law

It's a sad day, remembering Sandy
Campbell, one year ago, he passed away.
"Press on, regardless," he reminded me
"So we beat on, currents against the past"
68 miles, Whitney, Emily, Megan,
Slight incline, 214 feet
Towanda, Illinois, corn fields extend!
Cantaloupe at Recreation Plex, yes!
Historic Route 66 guides us on
I think we cycled 81 miles, wow!
Incredibly safe, Steve, Deb, as well
Alex kindly videotaped me,
As I wanted to say to Sandy,
Thank you, friend for all your love and guidance
Through Frost's words: nothing gold can stay.
So dawn goes down to day,
Nothing gold can stay.

> "Our greatest glory is not in never falling, but in getting up every time we fall." —Confucius

POEM 61: 26 JULY 2022
"Dwight, Illinois to Joliet, Illinois, 66 Miles"

Sweet home, Chicago, no, but, Joliet!
66 miles, heading toward Chicago
Wilmington, Illinois, we see a goose
Oh, my that's more than a goose, that's 20!
What a beautiful day, we lunch, laughing
Megan was cycling, just a couple days
There were many riders, but now, there's 5
Yes, cycling, Wauponsee, Glacial trail
In Joliet, there's Nauvoo, Illinois
Wauponsee was the Mormon Capital
Now, 2,289
Mormons, or 0.4 percent live there
Then, Joliet, Megan takes an Uber
"Blues Brother," con, a blessed event
But here now, Joliet, the old prison
Fenced in cages, barbed wire remains here
Hard metal steel walls still hold the spirit
So depressing, so dispiriting, sigh
Behind the steel fence, I am anxious here
I'm no prisoner, but as a black man
I wonder at the Old Joliet jail.
Reminder of the holocaust, sickening
In the car heading back, I ponder the words
"We're on a Mission from God;" I think not.

> "It's 106 miles to Chicago, we got a full tank of gas, half a pack of cigarettes, it's dark, and we're wearing sunglasses."
> —The Blues Brothers, 1980

POEM 62: 27 JULY 2022
Sweet Home, Chicago- "A Guardian Angel"

"For He will command His Angels" just you,
Cycling from Joliet to Chicago.
It was beautiful, pleasant, verdant trees,
He smiled and answered me, heliacal
As we rested and chatted as friends
And smiled and laughed, folding the taunt tents
Misery, however, was awaiting
Anxious, all six of us to Chicago,
The traffic, tight roads, hitting the potholes
Suddenly, thunder stroke, as we're trembling
Pouring raini, pleading for our frightened selves
But, he will command His Angels for us,
As he guided the narrow paths and loops
Home, safely, from tempestuous times
A friend, a guide, a young friendship for us.

POEM 63: 28 JULY 2022 (1)
"Gothic Art, the Beam, Chicago Event"

Yes, Chicago's legendary deep dish
George, Whitney, and Arlen, carry with us
Arrived at Ira J. Harris Hostel
Jackie, Whitney, George, and other ones
We can tour the museums with Michelle
Oh, yes, laundry day, red, whites, blues, washing
I walk, another protest, like Boulder
"Lorislalooza, curfew is racist"
Maybe a protest, but I walk to art
Michelle Millen arrives, smiling, sunny
We view Rodin's, The Burghers of Calais
Stoic, anguish, apathy, await fate
Impressionism, with Mary Cassatt
Art Institute of Chicago, home to
Georges Seurat, Sunday Afternoon
Vincent Van Gogh, self portrait watches us
Edward Hopper's "Nighthawks" glows in its frame
Of course, Grant Wood, "American Gothic,"
Spiritual borrowed pretentiousness
And of course, Winslow Homer, "Croquet Scene"
Winslow Homer, "Left, Right" a stroke, burden
And a statue President Abe Lincoln
A feast—feast—of steak salad with Sybil
Thank you, Frank and Sybil, it's wonderful!
The lovely park with Michelle, and the Bean
We travel to the Lake Shore Park event
Michelle, Susan Parker, Middlebury!

We walk Susan, Whitney, to the Towers
We dine with Susan by Lake Michigan
With a sunset and spectacular view
Chicago, that's our place, yes, Chicago

POEM 64: 28 JULY 2022 (2)
"Land of Lincoln"

I can remember, the land of Lincoln,
Cycling across the country, small, but large
Illinois is 1/6th of hundred days,
It's sunny, peaceful and flat stretching fields.
Cycling, across this America, too
For months, cycling, always cycling for land
Gentle riding now, through Litchfield, Springfield,
Goodfield, Odell, Joliet, quite gentle
Oh, yes, when traveling no winds, just sun!
Oh, Illinois, Chicago, Thunderstorms!
Yes, We're cycling across America,
America with deep-fried Oreos!
Thinking of Chicago, which is exciting:
Thunderstorms, wild traffic, The Bean, Grant Park
Legendary deep dish pizza, oh, yes!
Chicago Art Institute, Lake Shore Park
Or even, mayhap, Lalapalooza:
Maybe now, we shall never go home, friends
But, while cycling, we're looking for a home,
Cycling with cursed malady aphasia:
Destroys millions with disability
Of communication, not intellect.
We're fighting for recovery every day
Cycling, learning about ourselves, how far
We can push, what limits we overcome
Oregon and Washington, Montana,
Idaho, Wyoming, Colorado,
Nebraska, Kansas, and Missouri
We're cycling for beautiful Illinois,

Hoping, praying, for growth from aphasia:
"If costs you your peace, it's too expensive"
Practice, patience, prayer, it's all we can do.

POEM 65: 29 JULY 2022 (1)
"Route 66"

They come to 66, tributaries
The cultural icon, the "Mother Road"
Has been celebrated in film and song
Side roads, wagons, pleading trains and hobos,
And strength of all, with strong, sweet, shining sun
"In Medias res," in middle of things
We are cycling, Missouri, Illinois
Katy Trail State Park, a hard, but firm road,
Cycling, searing heat, but loving the shade
Great rain, wondrous torrents, but calm it is.
Under the Gateway Arch, we cycle east,
Route 66, or is it a bit north,
Placid Illinois, the land of Lincoln,
Good friend, Get your kicks on Route 66!
Cycling 88 is the migrant road
Some poor, some sad, some hitchhikers
But 66 is the path of people,
Yes, the most famous highway in the world!
You cycle even north, or even east,
And you arrive in windy Chicago,
Deep pan pizza, The Bean, Hancock tower,
Chi-town, American, America!
Yes, route 66, you've arrived, my friend.

POEM 66: 29 JULY 2022 (2)
Gary, Indiana

Gary in Lake County, Indiana,
63 miles, 22 feet rise up
I love cycling, summer, hot, beautiful!
Flat, smooth, sunny, pastoral campsite
Chicago, receding skyline away,
We cycle, Debra, Steve, Whitney, Arlen,
Gorgeous day, sunny goodbye, Chicago!
Those cities, Hammond, Gary, not Chicago
Gary Indiana, a proud City
'Course, "The Music Man," Meredith Wilson!
Professor Harold Hill, indeed, con man,
Purported a prosperous hometown
An alumnus '05, a great music room,
But later, he is revealed to lie!
What a tremendous show, "Music Man"!
And the revered Gary, Indiana,
In loving memory, Michael Jackson
We cycle and we love Lake Michigan,
As we cycle we're still moving, always,
"Our greatest glory is not never falling,
But in getting up every time we fall."
Confucius fuels me as we are cycling,
Speechless with aphasia, but I keep on.

POEM 67, 29 JULY 2022 (2)
"Indiana Dunes National Park"

The great parks, Yellowstone, and Grand Tetons
What a spectacular park, Wyoming
Gateway Arch National Park, Missouri
Three tremendous national parks cycling
There is a great one, 1966,
Indiana Dunes National Park, four!
50 miles of trails through shifting sand dunes
West Beach, Great Marsh, 15 miles of beaches
Me, I was exhausted from Chicago
We camped and we cycled, 63 miles
A Great National Park, but, I'm too tired
"Take the highway Lord knows I've been too long"
One time, on a sad days, sans Carolyn,
I'm cycling, 59 days, but, I miss her
I'm cycling, across this America
"But I'm heading east, heading towards her.

> *"One day you'll turn around and I'll be gone."*
> —The Marshall Tucker band

POEM 68: 30 JULY 2022
"Michigan City, IN to South Haven, MI"

George from Pennsylvania just loves cycling
He laughs, he smiles, he barks, he is joyful
He was in Montana, but now, he's back!
Now, Indiana, it's warm, no wind, yes!
Can you believe, 75 miles, 11 feet!
Town of Pines, dirtier than gravel, sigh
As we're cycling in Michigan City,
In great fear, for Nuclear Towers
Misconception: coal, gas, natural gas
Whitney took a smiling picture, "glowing?"
New Buffalo, Steve, Debra, George, Whitney
We cycle, George fixes his flat, a rest
Then, as we rise up to Lake Michigan
In summer, the beautiful lake, stunning
As crisp, as clear, as gentle, waves shimmer
Bright rays of the sun glisten the surface
Lunch, break, portrait, Steve, Debra, and Whitney
We pass by Whitney, cycling, where's Whitney?
I turn past, and I'm afraid: Whitney was hit
All those days, more than 60 days, I cried
All those times, cycling, I felt such numbing
Deprived of feeling, of responsiveness
We're waiting for how long, an hour, two?
We're cyclists, Stroke Across America
Deb and Steve cycle for 30 miles straight
We return, and I thought it was time, now
Whitney, my partner, returned with strapped arm
We can make it, Whitney, no matter what,

> *"To keep your balance, you must keep moving."*
> —Albert Einstein

POEM 69: 31 JULY 2022
"South Haven, Augusta, Michigan 52 Miles"

Debra, Steve, a friend named Val, are cycling
In Michigan, all are relatives, Deb
We cycle, only 206 feet
I like that, even though we're cycling sans Whitney
We arrive, a bit frustrated, and, wow!
Robin Pollens, gathers all of us for
Aphasia awareness, lunch, an event!
Communication enhancement program,
Aphasia, ACE, to help one another
I felt content, event, cycling across
We are close, Arlen, Steve, Debra, Whitney

> *"Now it springs up; do you not perceive it?*
> *I am making a way in the wilderness"*
> *Good company, good wine, good welcome,*
> *Can make good people."*
> —William Shakespeare

POEM 70, 1 AUGUST 2022
Augusta, to Concord, Michigan, 53 miles

Good company, good wine, good welcome, yes
We're cycling, Michigan, almost home
Ar least 12 events, plus Robin Pollens
Emily, Val, Steve, Deb, Emily, sweet
53 miles, 170 feet
An easy day, just cycling, lovely day
Smiles, everyone, Alex, Rusti, smiling
A group of friends, only 25 days
Cycling all day, and we camp out and wait
Monday afternoon, I call Zoom, Just ASK!
Denise Lowell, Aphasia, Stroke Knowledge
Writing my own poems, camping, loud music
Swains Lake Country Park Campground is busy.
Friendships will last forever, good welcome.

"Grapple them to thy soul with hoops of steel."
—William Shakespeare

POEM 71: 1 AUGUST 2022 (2)
"One"

Each morning, I awake, and I feel sore
Mine arms, on the left, and right side, tingle
Mayhap, I'm getting old each day, real fast,
But, perhaps, I had an ischemic stroke,
It has been six years, but I can feel it.
Mine arms, they are so weak, just look at it,
But, in my mental state, I fear pulling
When I awake, I find my left arm, tight,
I pull, hoping left arm will feel stronger
We can pray, after losing whole body
Squeezing in, squeezing out, but I still work
After an accident, my nose, broken,
And my whole self felt weakened: I too cried
Patience, practice, pray: that's all I can do.
So invisible, I walk, but, they know me,
Slightly limping, slightly erect—damnit!
Over 800,000 had a stroke,
Or, in just 40 seconds, you can crash.
Invisible, yes, but I had a stroke
Every day, each morning, I feel real sore
Sometimes I'm old, but, yes, it is a stroke
With my new arm, my new legs, weakening,
I'm anxious about my friends and my stroke:
"One life, one blood, but we're not the same," friend
With these anxiety and anxiousness,
I'm whelmed by these frustrations and sadness:
"Let your quiet mind listen and absorb,"
Because, "we get to carry each other"
Patience, practice, pray: that's all I can do.

POEM 72: 2 AUGUST 2022
"Concord, to Ann Arbor, MI 66 Miles"

With Alex and George, we're breathing, alive
"Happy to be alive, awake, breathing"
So opines George on the videotape
Breathe in, breathe out, that's all you can do
A spectacular day, and I await
"Happy to be alive, awake, breathing,"
So opines George on the videotape
In Jackson, Michigan, not Montana
Michigan, Jackson State Office Building
"Reserved Parking, registered vehicles"
We cycle, shoot, we're lost, but which way now?
"Excuse me, where's Revere Beach, Massachusetts?"
She looks puzzled: "Look over there, I guess"
We cycled toward Ann Arbor, Michigan.
Construction, turn left, turn right, no, that way
Ale, is smiling as we drove halfway
In Munich, we cycle the gravel path
Yes, "The rest we take between two deep breaths"
In Hamburg Township, we ride on asphalt
In Whitmore Lake, George, Alex, take a rest
"Stop, Pass With Care," admonished with us
It was hot, real hot, and we had to stop
We rode, got lost, of course, but found our way.
We met the family with a wild dog, yikes!
They settled down, it was okay, all right
We feasted on corn, chicken, and seltzer
The kids enjoyed swimming pool, superb spot
Northfield Township, we camped outside in tents
At night, coyotes howled and their prey cried.

I don't what it was, but, be careful, friends:
With a long sleep, I feel redivivus.

> *"Sometime the most important thing in a whole day is the rest we take between two deep breaths"* —Etty Hillesum, *An Interrupted Life, The Diaries 1941-1943*

POEM 73: 3 AUGUST 2022
Laundry, New Cycling Shoes, an Event

At breakfast with George, Arlen, and pancakes
We happily ask, "Where are we going?"
"Petri Bikes for your shoes; they are broken"
George, Arlen drive to Petri; it's awesome
Yes, they remake the new shoes, old fashioned
I put in the laundry, yes, reds, blues, orange
Swirling around, yet another event
My stars, all my clothes are new and ready!
Steve and Bill, what a nice home, tunes the bike
Thunder rumbles in the skies as I prepare
Erratic Ale Company welcomes us
Another event, "Identity Theft"
I share poems from my book, "Finding My Words"
In Dexter, Alex enjoys all the sounds
Over 30 persons, can speak and learn
Yes, thunderstorm pours for 15 minutes
And then it stops, again, like Wyoming
Steve, Debra, and Rusti, of course, listen
4,000 miles, that's an accomplishment!
Dr. Carol Persad from Michigan
Aphasia does not impact intellect
These events, this ride; I have a purpose
2,000 miles, yes, I have a purpose:
I'll ride, cold, rain, heat; I have a purpose
Whitney, Steve, Deb, Alex, Emily
We smile so profusely, what an event!

The storm: a reminder of the challenge.
"Have faith: the Lord will not abandon you"

> *"Dear young people, do not be afraid of making decisive choices in life. Have faith; the Lord will not abandon you!"*
> —Pope Francis

POEM 74: 4 AUGUST 2022
"Ann Arbor to Rochester, Michigan"

Arlen Hall always laughs; it keeps going
Toyota Rav 4, Arlen, 6 feet 4!
Debra, do you remember Michigan?
Debra, her homes, MIT, then Stanford
Then aphasia, paralyzed; now cycling
You've everything, Deb, because you are you
All of us, including your brother now!
Cycling, 39 miles, with broken trees
Oh, yes, there was a terrible storm,
All of our laundry, sleeping in the barn
At night, Jan Bennet quietly slept through
Now Bill, and others are cycling away.
Goodbye, Bill, his wife, and two little girls
In Volunteer Park, five of us, ready.
Ominous, cloudy, minacious: we'll ride
New Hudson, ten miles, a tree was fallen
Shrubs, trees, plants, branches, we'll have to climb it.
Under blinking lights, Deb and Steve made it.
Cycling 15 minutes, a tree fell down
No, not one tree, but two huge whole trees now!
At least seven bikes strewn across the path
Oh, it was still dripping beneath the trees
After an hour, we parked for our lunch
Erik, the documentarist, chatted
My blue Pearl Uzumi jacket muddy
We were soaked through, with our socks stained with mud
George, of course, reconfigured my shoes
We finished with Eric, the other one,
Yes, two documentarists in Auburn

We headed to the Detroit Tigers game
Comerica is a great stadium!
I love this place, baseball, "Black Lives Matter"
Arlen's Miguel Cabrera bobblehead.
Idealism, pragmatism: it shows

> *"Love is God's way, the moral way, but it's also the only thing that works. It's the rare moment where idealism actually overlaps with pragmatism."* —Michael B. Curry

POEM 75: 5 AUGUST 2022
An Event in Detroit, Corktown

Old shoes, just a pile of old shoes lie there
Battered, scraped from Montana, Wyoming,
Idaho, Colorado, Nebraska
Kansas, Missouri, Illinois cycling
Indiana, Michigan cycling still,
My torn, worn shoes now, are threading away
We're off to Auburn Hills Buffalo Wings
To enjoy barbecue, deep dish pizza
Guido's Pizza Premium Subs, too!
Whitney, Shawn, Dallas, Arlen, and Jan: friends.
We are family, I have to agree!
Detroit's deep dish pizza beats Chicago
We drive to Corktown, Detroit for event
I love this event, I have a purpose:
Crowds of stroke, aphasia, can give us all
Signing my poetry with my left hand!
Smiling Bruce Farrell was there, yes, Corktown
Dr. Carol Persad from Michigan,
Kait and Bruce enjoyed the Yard in Corktown
You won't believe it but, I hooked the ring!
My left hand keeps improving, my right, too.
These events: how we choose to spend our days
Learning, listening, telling our stories

> "It's what you've done with your time, how you've chosen
> to spend your days, and whom you've touched this year. .."
> —RJ Palacio

POEM 76: 6 AUGUST 2022
Rochester, MI to Algonac, MI 59 Miles

Setting off from the Holiday Express,
Arlen chuckles at the videotaped
59 miles, hot humid, but no rain
We cycled through the path and talked with friends
Oh, bother, another fallen tree path
20 minutes, another felled tree
From Washington to Romeo, trees down
Richmond, Arlen stops: let's have lemonade
Three kids are having the fun in summer
Richmond, 3 miles square and, yes, the mayor!
After we finished, I walked to the camp
Suddenly, I walk past this calm campsite:
"Hey, what are you doing? You must leave now!"
"I'm walking into the campsite, right there."
"No, you can't: you must go home right now—leave!"
"I'm going to the campsite, what's your problem?"
"You have to go now, or I will sic my dogs!"
Completely nonplussed, I gathered my bike
It was the only unsettling time, now
From Montana to Missouri and from
Illinois to Michigan, kindness.
Unsettling, but on to our campsite.
A nice dinner with ice cream, Apple Pay!
Seemingly spacious, expansive space,
Algonac, on the blue St. Clair River
Just a slight, small smidgen from Canada
Point Du Chêne, "Oak point," offers us cool shade

Next, I'll cycle, with close friends, Canada
My mind can expand, your mind can relax.

> *"When you ride a bike and you get your heart rate up and you're out, after 30 or 40 minutes, your mind tends to expand; it tends to relax."* —President George W. Bush

POEM 77: 7 AUGUST 2022

Let's add a traveller, Oh, Canada!
Cycling, five of us, a small crowd, rather
Jan, Steve, Deb, Alex, let's go, already!
Ferry to Canada, boy, I'm nervous
With Aphasia, showing my passport.
A small, intimate ferry, 6 persons
Smiles everyone, Jan, Steve, Deb, Alex
Land, ho! No problems, no questions, thank you!
"Nookshakaan," soften with body and weight
Alex, always smiling, travels the dirt path
We cycle, 50 miles, and Canada!
In a campsite, we shower, and we rest.

> *"Four wheels move the body, two wheels move the soul."*
> —Lani Lynn Vale

POEM 78: 8 AUGUST 2022
"*Morpeth, Ontario to Port Burwell, ON, 73 miles*"

Well, as long as I'm riding a bike,
Feeling lucky to be here with my friends.
We will cycle Port Burwell with the rain
Yes, we're cycling, and yes, it is pouring
73 miles, very flat 8 feet
Cycling, pouring, cycling: nothing to do
Yes, we rest in Kettle Creek Public School
Orange socks, dripping wet, my shoes, oh, pummeled,
Cycling through rain, and, finally, it's clear.
Finished one day in Canada, lucky!

> *"To me, it doesn't matter whether it's raining or the sun is shining or whatever: as long as I'm riding a bike, I know I'm the luckiest guy in the world."* —Mark Cavendish

POEM 79: 8 AUGUST 2022 (2)
Migraine, Right There

It's pouring, now, but cycling is my thing
The trail, anyone, Wyoming, Kansas,
It's Missouri, Michigan, Canada
Cycling today, and it's raining, pouring,
But, on the trail, I'm focused on gravel
Dirt, pebbles, shifts of minuscule rocks
It's unstable, yes, but now, I'm frightened:
Shifting pedal by pedal; it's raining
With tight hands, I can squeeze the handlebars.
I'm so afraid, speeding down a steep hill:
I'm so afraid, rising up a steep hill:
I'm so afraid, broken collar, snapped hip,
Each pedal is so tense, I can feel it.
The neck through my arms and throbbing migraine
You know the thin ice, when cycling—that's it!
I hope I don't slip, but the trail, okay
Well, "Nation shall rise against nation,"
But, as I cycle, let's hope I don't fall.

POEM 80: 9 AUGUST 2022
Port Burwell, Canada, Laundry, 0 miles

On Tuesday morning, it's laundry today
Towels, blue Pearl Uzumi, orange shirt, socks
A quiet day, then, Alex rides the tandem
With Steve, Alex laughing all the way
Arlen, Emily, Alex, Jan, Whitney
Debra, my heroine, and Steve, were there
We feasted on mussels for our dinner.
Rare for dessert, but I had apple pie!
The ship, HMCS Ojibwa
A looming submarine, a museum
It's one of the most unique attractions!
Yes, yet another across our journey
The road's long with many stories to tell.

> *"Just because someone carries it well, doesn't mean it it's heavy."* —Anonymous

POEM 81: 10 AUGUST 2022
Port Burwell to Port Dover, 44 Miles

LL Cool J, says, "Don't call it comeback"
Recovered from her spill, Whitney will ride.
Hallelujah, Whitney, my partner, rides
Arlen warily watches, Whitney rides
20 miles, she's so excited, she smiles!
Lake Erie is a magnificent lake
3/5ths of the Great Lake Michigan
Emily leads with a great, waving flag
And yes, Whitney, my partner, my good friend
Port Dover, a spectacular home
Deb, Steve, Whitney, Jan, Arlen, Alex
And Emily, smiling, serves our salmon
I can imagine such a close knit kin
"Be a rainbow in someone else's cloud."

"Be a rainbow in someone's else's cloud." —Maya Angelou

POEM 82: 11 AUGUST 2022
Port Dover, to Dunville Ontario, 49 miles

15 days, it's Canada, I'm happy!
Jan, Whitney, Debra, Steve, Alex, we ride.
Cycling, 49 miles, and it is gorgeous!
I can realize, yes, I will be here soon
Those days, with unseasonable weather,
I can see clearly now is rain is gone
We smile, so expectant, so exciting!
Nanticoke, Lake Erie, so beautiful
Hogweed, glandular globe thistle, cycling
Goldilocks aster, St, John's-wort, riding
In Selkirk, Steve and Debra are cycling
Laughing, all the way, isn't it lovely?
We stop at Selkirk for a photo op:
Robots, Bernie Sanders in his mittens.
Jan, smiling now, really enjoys herself
Signposts pointing to Beijing, San Paulo
At lunch, Steve, Deb, Whitney, Jan, and Alex,
Enjoying wet, sloppy, sweet, sweet melons
Deb loves melons, and Whitney eats some too
"Do the pokey and you turn yourself about,"
That's what it's all about in Canada.
We cycle, on the the rough, gravelly stones
Jan exits and we cycle, smoothly, "home"
We laugh and play, and return for campsite
It's all about life and happiness

POEM 83: 11 AUGUST 2022
Thinking back: where we've been

"Sadness hurts, but it's a healthy feeling,"
I listen, intently, as I hear this:
Cycling in Montana, yes, relentless,
Climbing hundreds of hills, perspiring,
As I push, pull, tug: what am I doing?
It gave sadness, but it made me feel good:
In Idaho, freezing in Jackson Hole,
6,237 feet:
35 degrees, I pulled, tugged my glove,
I cycled: will I make it? It's cold,
I made it, God bless us: I know, sadness
Wyoming, torrents of winds of fury,
Oh, yes, I cycled, winds of 40 miles,
How can it be, Zephyrs, laughing,
Colorado over Cameron pass!
10,276 feet!
With mountains, with rain, with sirens, Kansas
Together above, yes, even Kansas,
We cycle to ride, to feel, to yearn;
Sometimes the ride is kind, gentle, Missouri,
Katy Trail State Park, with gravel and shade.
With Illinois, Chicago, thunderstorms,
Laughing, dancing, just loving it, too,
But 100 days grow closer, yes, now,
We cycle Indiana, Michigan
Each one closer, and we are now tighter
Canada, whelming storms and pouring rain,
The days bring us closer to the sad end
"Sadness hurts, but it's a healthy feeling."

Having adventure, loving all of us.
Every day, beating back this nasty stroke.
It's sadness, but only the last full days:
This cycling across America ride:
The riding, the struggle, makes us feel close
I can be depressed, but there is gladness
Friends, together we can overcome this
Just by living the full life, day by day.

POEM 84: 12 AUGUST 2022
Canada

O, Canada, our home and native land,
From Algonac, Michigan 50 miles,
We cycled to the small border ferry.
"Passport, please," yes, aphasia, nervous
"Nookshaan" or "Stop:" welcome O, Canada!
Cycling, mirific, cycling our wonders
We love this now, cycling across the world
Morpeth, Port Burwell, Port Dunville, so clear
Cycling, sun, every day, I'm almost there
Elevation, five days, 210'!
73 miles, Morpeth, stunning, but rain.
O, Canada, we stand on guard for thee!
Canada, such beautiful lakes abound.
Riders together, we are family,
Dinners with questions glue us together:
"Is there a God?" "Who is your family?"
Cycling from Montana to Canada.
It feels different now, the bond between us.
Only a few months, but we are family.

POEM 85: 12 AUGUST 2022 (2)
"Dunville, Ontario to Buffalo, New York 40 miles"

"But I trust you, Lord, I say you're my God"
40 single small miles, to Buffalo!
Everyone's giddy, yes, Jan, Emily
Debra, Steve, Whitney, America, yes!
Port Colborne, in Canada, still sparkling
Jan, a determined, serious cyclist,
Smiles, beautifully, on this sunny day
Whitney, of course, my partner, is smiling
We rest for break with Waverley Park
Goodbye, Whitney, Jan, Emily, Deb, Steve
Fort Erie Beach, cycling towards Buffalo
With patience, Emily entrances us
With Deb and Steve, we climb over the fence
"Todos, los viajeros", we arrived!
We cycled through the streets, hey, Buffalo!
Drink up, the Anchor Bar Buffalo Wing
Joan Rice, my Middlebury College friend.
And, of course, Buffalo Wings, well, all right!
We met Debra and Kathy O'Leary!
We talked about Steve, Deb and the tandem
What a great evening with my cycling friends
And, of course, Happy Birthday, Emily!
You are pleasant, kind, gentle, sunny!
Only 14 days, can you believe it?
"But I trust you, Lord, I say you're my God"

poem 86: 13 august 2022
Event, Buffalo, New York

The essence of leadership is Steve
Since youth, Steve desired cycling across
The country but other things- three children
And living life deferred the dream for time
Then, Debra's stroke, and determination
Identity Theft, Stroke Onward, and SAAM.
Now, Steve and Deb organized a cycling trip
Astoria, Revere Beach; he'll make it
Now, Deb and Steve, speak in Buffalo.
Steve, you are a hero, because you'll lead
"The heroes are those who make peace and build"

> *"The heroes are those who make peace and build."*
> —Nelson Mandela

POEM 87: 14 AUGUST 2022
"Buffalo to Niagara Falls, 34 miles"

Wow, 5 cyclists to 11 cyclists
Em's father will ride Niagara Falls
Em, Andy, her father, are excited!
Yes, passport through Canada to U.S.
Niagara River, just beautiful
Niagara Falls, wonder of the world
Adventure pack, incredible views
Cave of the winds, descend gorge, feel water
I've been thrice, but this time, spectacular
The grandeur of Creator's power!
Trembling, I reach the Niagara Falls
It's tremendous, and I thank God for life.
Alex, Emily, Steve, Debra, Whitney,
He definitely exists for wonders
In the rainbow and the sparkling mist.

> "Their roar is around me. I am on the brink Of the great waters—and their anthem voice Goes up amid the rainbow and the mist." — Grenville Mellen

POEM 88: 15 AUGUST 2022
Erie Canal

Niagara Falls great time, Spencerport
Cycling with Arlen, 10 miles in August
Okay, flat tire, call up RV, please
Arlen, ever patient, waiting for bike
Steve and Debra ride with, of course, Rusti
While waiting, we peer under the barges
With the stern statues, Arlen takes pictures
Lockport remembers and celebrates
Labored 12-hour days, April, November
Navigate the freight Buffalo to west
And to New York City and points south
The Lock Tenders statues and photographs
For posterity, Arlen pushed the beam!
With Lockport and Medina, cycling
Yes, the Erie Canal, gavel and path
"She's a good old worker and good old pal,"
15 miles on the Erie Canal, yes!
Alex, smiling, bien sûr, cycled "the falls"
Covering the camp, we find this flat path
Go, fight for the things that you care about.

POEM 89: 16 AUGUST 2022
Spencerport to Clyde, NY 68 Miles

Life, sometimes, can be fun, can be finished
Arise, friend, this morning, you have 10 days
I packed up my tent, had breakfast, cycling
Memories, even of Rusti, 2 months!
In Sweden, Steve and Deb pulled up with Jan
On Erie Canal, cycling gravel path
Missouri, Illinois, Indiana
so many miles, yet, still, we are cycling
It feels good; yes, 16 miles per hour!
I made it, one day, a small achievement!
Dallas smiles, as we stop to share ice cream.
Reminds me of Missoula, Montana
Shawn telling me that was the best ice cream.
Can you imagine, two long months ago?
Now, two months later, enjoying ice cream in New York.
In Tyre, New York, at the campsite, we dine.
A comfortable night, reading some Thoreau
It feels nice, and it all feels connected,
How beautiful it is to be unbroken.

"How beautiful it is to be unbroken." —Mary Oliver

POEM 90: 17 AUGUST 2022

Funny, but, you have to laugh: mosquitoes
It's summer, we're cycling, my arms itching.
Construction on Centerport Aqueduct
Historic New York, The Erie Canal,
Greatest engineering accomplishment.
On the 4th of July 1817
Leadership, Governor De Witt Clinton
Blasted, 363 mile
They hewed the solid rocks and the marshes
83 locks in 1825
Connecting Albany to Buffalo,
From Atlantic Ocean to The Great Lakes
A wonder of the world, a genius build!
The Canalway Trail, Jordan, marvel site!
Syracuse, Onondaga Lake Park
Arlen and I stop for tea, McDonald's
At a campsite, Fayetteville, reunion
With friends Chris and Diana, 30 years
We celebrate their anniversary
With barbecue and many, many laughs
Delicious, smooth ice cream caps our visit.
We depart ways; it's only 9 days now

"Why can't a bicycle stand up by itself? Because it's two-tired."

POEM 91: 18 AUGUST 2022
Bridgeport, NY to Herkimer, NY 63 Miles

Green Lakes State Park, and boy, I'm excited
8 days to go, and Whitney, my partner,
And Emily, oh, yes, Jan's cycling, too
It's a perfect day, and Erie Canal
Durhamville, New York, and Steve, Debra rest
Rusti, with a fuller coat, snacks bit
In Oriskany, Jan stops, points out a snake!
Jan loves cycling and notices nature.
Jan stops and takes a picture, a turtle!
She smiles so much at the turtle, close up!
Jan, that captures the essence of summer
Beautiful ride, 63 miles, enjoy.
Summertime and the living is easy.

POEM 92: 19 AUGUST 2022
Event, Albany: Carolyn will be there!

"Pedal, breathe, repeat. I will see my wife—soon"
Emily, an intern from Wash U,
Created an event for Albany
I'm so honored, so blessed, so humbled:
Thank you, Emily and Alex, you're stars!
Laundry, of course, orange, blue Pearl Uzumi
Relaxing day, heading for Albany
We drive 80 miles, and I'm excited!
Welcome, friends, Stroke Across America
Rusti wears Stroke Across America
Yes, Carolyn talks to me every day
But, from Lolo to now, we've been apart.
I hug Matt Murnane from Academy
Then, Stroke Survivor, I kiss Carolyn!
There's Kirk Harbinger from Academy
A photographer from Channel 13
Adam Eliot, friend from fifth grade, rode
His motorcycle from New York City!
Chis McEnroe, best friend, drove from Marion
Jim Poole, '68, former track and field
Steve and Debra shared our event, New York
Carolyn spoke of changes to our lives
Aphasia, an unexpected hard turn.
My sister, Heather, my nephew, Christian
Colby, my nephew, and Krissy, as well
Todd Van Deak, the SLP was there
And my old friend, Kevin Scullen joined us.
Such a tremendous night in Albany.
Pedal, breathe, repeat: I will see my wife- soon.

POEM 93: 20 AUGUST 2022
Herkimer NY to Schenectady NY, 66 Miles

252 miles left for one week
Yes, cycling, but it gets bigger, better
All along, people cycling with us now,
Then, Montana, 12 persons, but now 10
Arlen, others, photographers, Beth, Steve, Jan
Debra, Emily, Alex, and Dallas,
Whitney- my partner- Tony, and, Rusti
66 miles, relatively flat road
Yes, Happy Anniversary, Deb!
Carolyn and I hug goodbye and part.
It's beautiful, flat roads to German Flatts
Just like Montana and Indiana
Fort Plain, New York, lovely, spectacular
Always cycling, pass by the horse and buggy
In Sprakers, New York, bike pathers welcome
I rest and gird myself for 35 miles
Florida, New York, stopping for our lunch
We cycle through Schohaire Crossing
Historic site on the Erie Canal
Long day, 66 miles, Pattersonville
Found that hill, 646 feet
Jan, Tony, Alex through Schenectady
Deb, Steve, Happy anniversary.
We arrive at Frosty Acres campground.
166 miles: Hold on, I'm coming.

"Find ecstasy in life; the mere sense of living is joy enough."
—Emily Dickinson

POEM 94: 21 AUGUST 2022
Schenectady to Castleton, NY, 47 Miles

It's closer, New York to Massachusetts
"True hope is swift and flies with swallow wings"
Opines William Shakespeare, almost each day!
Deb, Steve, Whitney- my partner- Beth, cycling
Only 47 miles, can you feel it?
Jeff Blatnik Park, Niskayuna, cycling
It's clear, it's nice, it's seemingly flat
The Mohawk River glides beside our path.
It is so majestic, so beautiful,
Then, I can see it, The Corning Towers!
Albany's here; my mother raised me there!
18 years, Albany Academy
The past's memories, a thought arising
Corning City Preserve, Heather, Christian,
My sister, nephew, Christian and Krissy
Hugs with family and then went on
We cycle to a hotel, Castleton
16 people for a smiling dinner!
We've grown now, 16 people, holy cow!
In retrospect these years of hard struggle,
Will strike you as the most beautiful, yes.

> *"One day in retrospect the years of struggle will strike you as the most beautiful."* —Sigmund Freud

POEM 95: 21 AUGUST 2022 (2)
New York

New York, New York, it's a wonderful town
It's Niagara Falls and Buffalo, too
Visiting with friends, family, and you
Almost home, yes, Montana gone
Idaho, freezing with snow, Wyoming,
Incredulous of winds, sensational
Cycling mountains; next, there, Colorado
Cycling, lurching, cautious, disbelieving,
As sirens with Roman mythology,
Dangerous, sea creatures, enchanting songs,
Half-bird, half creatures, lure sailors to deaths
Similar with beards, with songs, or daemons:
Not me, Colorado, mountains cycling,
The truth symbolizes against sea and me
Cameron Pass, this Siren, engaging,
I made it, but that was two months ago,
Nebraska, Kansas, Missouri, cycling
Illinois, Indiana, cycling,
Michigan, Canada, amazing storms
But, now, I made it, almost -New York
I can feel it, taste it; cycling to go,
Beautiful paths and canal myths,
Niagara Falls was spectacular,
Buffalo's event was spectacular
Guiding stars, above us, like mythic leaders
Aphasia stroke, praising tandem cycle
Lockport, canals, cycling 55 miles,
Syracuse, Sweden with those those mythic names
Centerport, Aqueduct Park, and Jordan

Cycling 91 days, ever closer
Emily sequestered with Rusti, laughing
Onondaga Park, unusually small,
Well, Syracuse, but these are closer now,
Green Lakes State Park with Diana, Chris
10 full days, but we loved those New York days.
Jan, Alex, Emily, Debra and Steve
91 days: we're very close knit now.
Weaving and sewing, Arlen, Shawn, and Jan
16 events, Buffalo, Albany
Tremendous times with Carolyn, my wife
Almost 65 days, tired, skinny.
Yes, now, 93 days, Excelsior
Yes, an apocryphal siren is gone.

POEM 96: 22 AUGUST 2022
Castleton, NY to Pittsfield, MA 39 Miles

Small wins to break down big, difficult goals
Small wins, diversity and inclusion
Turn less daunting and more achievable
Over 13 persons from East Greenbush
Attractive place in an idyllic site
Cycling, smiling, such a staggering set
Howie, gosh, haven't seen since Montana
We rest in East Chatham, waiting, New York
Steve, Deb, smiling, over 4,000 miles!
East Chatham to Richmond, Massachusetts!
Zero miles, hallelujah, I'm coming!
Cunningham Hill, welcome, Massachusetts
So many places, Market Place, Pittsfield
Whitney- partner- Arlen, Steve, Deb, Alex
Our campsite, almost there, we met a man
He spoke about his dog and cycling
He gave us $50, but that was kind
In so many travels, places, small wins:
I know: focusing on small wins is hard
To do it, always, is impossible
I try the large goal and then I am lost;
Rather than the small forward step I take,
I find the small things, the unbroken steps,
Challenge yourself, the fragility of life,
Small wins each one, cycling across New York.

> *"Every day, I'm hustlin', hustlin', hustl—"*
> —William Roberts, Jermaine Jackson, Andrew Harr, (Rick Ross)

POEM 97: 23 AUGUST 2022
Pittsfield to Northhampton, MA, 50 miles

In Scotland, I heard of a Hairy COO
But, it's only a regular cow, moo!
Cycling up, 50 miles to Northhampton
Many people cycling now, what's your name?
It's raining, since Canada, there's a storm,
Ah, yes, "Blow winds, and crack your cheeks! Rage blow
You cataracts and hurricanoes, spout
Till you have drenched our steeples, drowned the cocks.
You sulph'rous and thought-executing fires,"
Ah, King Lear, remember climbing, burning
Cameron Pass and now climbing again.
Again: 1,106 feet
Montana, Wyoming were easier.
Quick, shot, steep hills, terrifying downhill
Oh, and then the rain, Debra says, patience
It rained slowly, and we cycled through Leeds
Ah, Massachusetts, the bicycle path
We stopped, we met Marion Patterson!
In Northhampton, we shared with 6 persons,
Chip, Susan, Guy, Isabella and friends,
Susan, my sister-in-law, met Rusti!
A great time, Happy birthday, Alex!
"And let's not be weary in well doing,"
Let us remember, we still have 3 days.

POEM 98: 24 AUGUST 2022
North Hampton, MA to West Brookfield, MA

As if I were performance, we're cycling
38 miles, lots of fun performances
I hug Steve's mother, visiting us
We cycle through Elwell Island and wow,
Amherst College, Sara's Deb's mom, daughter
Then, Belchertown, Massachusetts, cycling
A break, it's stunning, Quabbin Reservoir
We rest a bit, and it is beautiful
1930 to 1939,
The reservoir was built in the U.S.
Remember, The New Deal, WPA?
We took picture with smiling 9 persons
We cycled with Debra, Steve, and Rusti
In Northhampton, we sat, Stroke Support Group
Number 14 event, UMASS, Amherst
What a lovely evening, and then dinner
14 persons; it grows larger each time;
Rejoice in hope, be patient with great love

> "Rejoice in hope, be patient in tribulation, be constant in prayer." —2. Romans 12:12

POEM 99: 25 AUGUST 2022
West Brookfield, MA to Concord, MA, 55 Miles

99 days, Steve and Deb, amazing
With a Herculean task, we will do this
Alex smiles in the video, as I climb
On the videotape, Kim said, "It's awesome!
"It's an amazing ride, and all of you!"
Cycling now, 10,15 of us, Bolyston
At Hudson, we have lunch and rest with owls
We pass Caty and Nat Kessler's nice home
Concord, holds a significant place
In the history of America.
Revolutionary War started here!
It's a lovely night with Caty and Nat,
So gracious, so kind are Caty and Nat
Deb, my heroine, is magnificent
Deb playfully tugs away the Red Sox hat!
Capturing Deb's always playful spirit
Celebration with Steve, Debra, Whitney
At least 20 persons to celebrate
The 99th day from spring to summer
With all humility and gentleness
And patience and love, we are together

> *"With all humility and gentleness, with patience, bearing with one another in love."* —Ephesians 4:2

POEM 100: 26 AUGUST 2022
Massachusetts

"I'm going back to Massachusetts,"
Bee Gees song plays in my mind as I ride.
This state: 143 miles
But the steep hills were my final challenge.
Climbing upwards, first, and searing downwards
The extremely, intense August, yes, home
Cycling from Pittsfield to Revere Beach
Home, going, coming, from Massachusetts
Only six days, but they were long and hot.
Sehnsucht, longing, yearning to arrive home.
The hills were challenging, but somehow, home
The views were spectacular, but still,
Montana, Idaho, far, far, away,
Wyoming, Jackson, mountains were stunning,
Colorado, memories of hard grit,
Nebraska, Kansas, half way miles away
Missouri, Illinois, Indiana,
9 more states away, yes, I'm hustling now!
Michigan, Canada, New York, it's good:
But Massachusetts I could, feel, taste it.
And then, Revere Beach, yes, the final rest
It moves you, feels you, needs you, greets you- home
A mist of ocean air, salt water,
Don't cry because it's over, smile because
It happened: 3,383 miles
Yes, "they shall mount up with wings as eagles"
Feels like going back to Massachusetts

"But they that wait upon the Lord shall renew their strength; they shall mount up with wings as eagles, they shall run and not be weary, and they shall walk and not faint." —Isaiah 40:31

POEM 101
Revere Beach

"Those who hope in the Lord will renew their strength"
Concord, Massachusetts to Revere Beach
Sometimes only 4 cycling, now, hundreds
Oh, yes, we are soaring on eagle's wings.
Cycling, traffic, gorgeous day, 30 miles
Lexington, Great Meadows, cycling always
Stop, rest; Minuteman Bike path, Arlington
Davis Square, now Revere, are we there yet?
My unspeakable love there, Carolyn:
Cycling, Montana to Revere, my wife
Finally, Arlen smiles, rests my shoulder,
"You're done, Michael, friend, congratulations."
"I'm done, truly, I'm done?" I wept, crying.
3,383 miles
Steve, Debra, Whitney, and I walk ahead:
Into the Atlantic Ocean, bikes high.
Dozens of friends and family, watch us
I dip into the ocean, waves embrace.
The sand, the salt, the sun welcomes me home
"They'll run and not be weary, they will walk and not be faint."
I did it it, from Montana to Revere
"Peace I leave with you; peace I give you."

EPILOGUE:
Ode to Steve and Debra

Tell me the one, who, Steve and Debra
The Cyclist blown off course time and again
They cycled, Oregon, Massachusetts:
Speak again, Steve and Debra, you are loved
You cycled 4,500 miles
147,000 feet,
Always searching the mind that could be lost:
Washington, Oregon, Montana,
Cycling, always cycling, YES, EFI
That's every Friendly Inch, moving, cycling
Of all the cities, they saw, aa of it
First, Missoula, Montana, Littleton
Kansas City, St. Louis, Chicago,
Detroit, Buffalo, Albany, Boston!
We loved Every Friendly Inch, and cycled:
Speak, memory, of the cunning hero,
Who smiled, cheerful, and optimistic,
Laughing at the rains, the rains pouring us,
I,m singing in the rain, loving it all!
Steve, remember, lollipop incident
You, someone who had changed course of our lives
With a moment of Simple and kindness:
And with Debra, beautiful Debra,
She's beautiful, but she is aphasia,
Cursed one with the tangled web we weave
12 years, battling, searching, spitting it out,
A forceful, seemingly violent to win
No "it matters not how strait the gate" feels
And "How Charged the punishments" she works

Because with aphasia, *she wills it,* knows
Debra, your head is bloody, but unbowed:
800,000 people are stoke now,
Or every 40 seconds, pummeled
But, Debra fights. Every day she fights
Debra, I am woman, hear me roar!
She is the master of my fate, *She'll win*:
*Speak, great Steve, with a c*aregiver with her,
Tell, Steve and Deb, see ev'ry word and sites
And tell the brave tale once more in our time
How, together, we advocate for us,
Cycling Across America, this time
So we can fight, and the storm, to win
From the Pacific, to Astoria
To the Atlantic dipped in the Revere:
Ah, yes, Speak Memory, to feel so good,
In our world, with strong winds and favored friend

Scan this QR code with your phone to see a Google Photos album from the trip.

MICHAEL OBEL-OMIA is a public speaker, writer, and educator who has lived with aphasia since a stroke in 2016. In his ongoing journey of recovery, he found inspiration in poetry—a medium that allows him to express what speech cannot. A passionate advocate for stroke survivors and individuals with aphasia, Michael has published numerous essays and a compelling collection of poetry titled *Finding My Words: Aphasia Poetry*. He lives in Barrington, Rhode Island, with his wife Carolyn, whose support continues to inspire his voice and vision.

www.ingramcontent.com/pod-product-compliance
Lightning Source LLC
Chambersburg PA
CBHW071119160426
43196CB00013B/2629